YORK NOTES

General Editors: Professor A.N. Jeffares (*University of Stirling*) & Professor Suheil Bushrui (*American University of Beirut*)

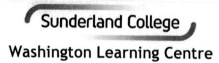

YORK PRESS
Immeuble Esseily, Place Riad Solh, Beirut.

LONGMAN GROUP UK LIMITED
Longman House, Burnt Mill, Harlow,
Essex CM20 2JE, England
Associated companies, branches and representatives
throughout the world

First published 1980
Ninth impression 1993

ISBN 0-582-78161-2

Produced by Longman Singapore Publishers Pte Ltd
Printed in Singapore

Contents

Part 1

Introduction

Geoffrey Chaucer

Not very much is known of Chaucer's life. Even the exact date of his birth is unknown, but Chaucer when giving evidence at a trial in 1386 admitted to being 'forty years old and more.' Also, he was old enough to be a soldier in 1359. A date of 1343 or 1344 for his birth is therefore a reasonable guess.

Chaucer's father, John Chaucer, was a prosperous wine-merchant, whose services were employed on several occasions by King Edward III (1327–77). Geoffrey's first employment was as a page-boy in the service of Elizabeth, Countess of Ulster, whose husband, Prince Lionel, was a son of King Edward. Chaucer held this post in 1357. In 1359–60 he took part in the wars with France, being taken prisoner near Reims. King Edward contributed £16, a large sum at that time, to his ransom, and must therefore have valued his services highly.

About 1366, Chaucer married Philippa Swynford. Her sister Katherine was the mistress, and later the wife, of John of Gaunt, another son of King Edward. Chaucer was thus a friend and brother-in-law of one of the most powerful men in the kingdom. One of Chaucer's early poems, *The Book of the Duchess*, was written in 1369 to commemorate the death of John of Gaunt's first wife Blanche.

From 1368 onwards Chaucer was employed several times on diplomatic missions in Europe. In 1372 he travelled to Genoa, in Italy, to negotiate a commercial contract with the Genoese. On this occasion he also visited Florence, the literary centre of Italy. This journey may have provided him with his first contact with Italian literature which, as we shall see, greatly influenced his own writing.

In the course of his life Chaucer held a number of posts in the public service, including those of Controller of Customs in the port of London, Member of Parliament and Clerk of the King's Works. He died on 25 October 1400, and was buried in Westminster Abbey, where his tomb may still be seen.

The official records show that Chaucer was a diplomat and a shrewd man of affairs. They never mention the fact that he was also a prolific and accomplished poet. He was indeed the greatest English poet of his time. The most important of his many writings are *Troilus and Criseyde*, written about 1385, and *The Canterbury Tales*, a collection of stories of which *The Franklin's Tale* forms a part. *The Canterbury Tales* was still unfinished at the time of Chaucer's death.

The French background

In 1066 William, Duke of Normandy in Northern France, invaded England and made himself King William I. He is often referred to as 'William the Conqueror.' His accession to the throne made an enormous impact on all aspects of English life, including English literature.

William brought to an end the Old English ('Anglo-Saxon') civilisation. He suppressed the native English aristocracy, replacing it with Norman-French noblemen. For the next three hundred years, French taste exercised a dominating influence on English culture. The royal court, and indeed most of the more powerful people in England, spoke French rather than English. Very little literature of merit was produced in the English language.

There was however a flourishing literary tradition in England in the twelfth and thirteenth centuries. It was not written in the English language. Literature intended to entertain and amuse would be written in French. More scholarly literature—religious, philosophical, scientific or historical works—would be written in Latin, which was understood by all educated people.

In the latter part of the twelfth century there lived in England a woman called Marie. She had come from France, and is therefore referred to as *Marie de France*. She wrote among other things a set of short love-stories in French verse. She called them *lais*, and claimed that they were translations from songs in Breton, the language of Brittany in north-west France. It is quite possible that she was not telling the truth. At this time, writers often claimed that their works were translations from another language, rather than original compositions. This was a literary convention. Certainly, no songs of the kind Marie describes have survived in the original Breton.

Marie had many imitators. The 'Breton Lay' became a popular *genre*. People would write stories, usually on the theme of love, set either in Brittany or in Great Britain. Like Marie they would claim, either at the beginning or at the end of their story, that it was a translation of a song composed by Breton minstrels. Such a claim is made by the Franklin in *The Franklin's Tale*. It is not, however, to be taken seriously. *The Franklin's Tale* is a translation, with many alterations, of a story by the Italian writer Boccaccio.

During the fourteenth century, the English language gradually regained its position as the main literary language of England. In the north and west of England, there was a revival of the kind of poetry written before the accession of William the Conqueror. This was in *alliterative* verse: that is, the lines are not of any fixed length, but several words in the line begin with the same sound. The poem *Sir Gawain and the Green Knight* is a product of this 'alliterative revival'.

But in the south-east, where Chaucer lived, French influence was stronger. Poets did not use the ancient alliterating line, but took new verse-forms copied from French models. They used a fixed number of syllables (usually eight or ten) to a line, and linked the lines together by rhyme. The ten-syllable rhyming lines which Chaucer uses in *The Franklin's Tale* are common in English poetry before this century.

English poets took not only their verse-forms, but also their subject-matter, from French literature. French poets wrote, above all, about love between men and women. Sexual love, a subject which had occurred only rarely in the Old English poetry written before William the Conqueror, is frequently treated in Middle English literature. It is the subject of *The Franklin's Tale* and many other Canterbury Tales.

Often in medieval French love-literature, and in the English love-literature deriving from it, a young man is depicted as suffering extreme pain because of his feelings for a woman. She is said to have 'wounded' his heart. He may believe himself to be in such pain that he will surely die. Thus, in one of the 'Breton Lays' of Marie de France, the hero Guigemar finds himself in this condition:

> But love had mortally wounded him. Now his heart was in great distress, for the lady has so wounded him that he has forgotten his native country.

In this tradition the man often falls in love with the woman at first sight. The woman is said to have wounded his heart through his eyes. Thus, in a story by the twelfth-century French poet Chrétien de Troyes, the knight Yvain looks out of a window and sees the woman whose husband he has just killed. The effect is immediate:

> His enemy has his heart, he loves the being who hates him most. The lady has well avenged the death of her lord, and does not know it. She has taken a greater vengeance than would have been possible had not Love avenged her, gently attacking him through the eyes and wounding his heart. And this wound lasts longer than the wound of a lance or a sword. A sword wound is cured and soon healed when the doctor attends to it, but the wound of Love grows worst when it is nearest to its doctor.

Similarly in Chaucer's poem *The Knight's Tale*, which, like *The Franklin's Tale*, is part of *The Canterbury Tales*, a young man receives a shock when he looks out of a window:

He cast his eye upon Emelya
And therwithal he bleynte and cride, 'A!'
As though he stongen were unto the herte.

(He cast his eye upon Emily, and at that he started back and cried 'Ah!' as if he were wounded to the heart.)

In this tradition the love-sick young man will often be afraid to tell the woman of his feelings for her. Instead, he may retire to his bed for a year or two in great discomfort. Thus in *The Knight's Tale* the young man's sufferings are described in these terms:

His slep, his mete, his drynke, is hym biraft,
That lene he wex and drye as is a shaft;
His eyen holwe, and grisly to biholde,
His hewe falow and pale as asshen colde,
And solitarie he was and evere allone,
And waillynge al the nyght, makynge his mone;
And if he herde song or instrument,
Thanne wolde he wepe, he myghte nat be stent.
So feble eek were his spiritz, and so lowe,
And chaunged so, that no man koude knowe
His speche nor his voys, though men it herde.

(He can no longer sleep or eat or drink, so that he became as lean and dry as a shaft of wood. His eyes were sunken, and horrible to look at. His colour was yellow, and pale as cold ashes. He spent all his time alone, wailing and complaining all night. And if he heard a song or a musical instrument he would weep, there was no stopping him. His spirits also were so feeble and low, so different from normal, that no man would recognise his voice if he heard it.)

This 'lovers' malady' is known as *Hereos* (from the Greek *Eros*, meaning Love). It afflicts Aurelius, the young squire of *The Franklin's Tale*:

In langour and in torment furyus
Two yeer and moore lay wrecche Aurelyus.

(In sickness and in furious torment wretched Aurelius lay for two years and more.)

The lover is often said in this tradition to be completely in the power of his lady. He is her slave; she has the power of life and death over him. Thus, in Chrétien de Troye's story of Yvain, the hero has killed the lady's husband. He speaks to her as follows:

'Lady, truly, I will not seek your mercy, but rather I will thank you for whatever you wish to do to me, because nothing you do could displease me.'

'No, sir? And what if I kill you?'

'My lady, if it please you, you will never hear me speak against it.'

'Never', she said, 'have I heard of such a thing, that you voluntarily put yourself completely in my power, without compulsion.'

'Lady, there is no force so strong, truly, as that which commands me to submit absolutely to your will.'

This force, of course, is Love. In the same way Arveragus, the knight in *The Franklin's Tale*, agrees to obey his lady Dorigen; likewise the squire Aurelius throws himself entirely on his lady's mercy.

The Italian background

Chaucer visited Italy at least twice, and was acquainted with the work of the leading Italian writers Dante (1265–1321), Petrarch (1304–74) and Boccaccio (1313–75). There is a tradition that Chaucer met Petrarch, though this is not certain. Several of Chaucer's poems are adaptations of works by Boccaccio. Chaucer's great work *Troilus and Criseyde* is an adaptation of Boccaccio's *Il Filostrato*; *The Knight's Tale* is derived from Boccaccio's *Teseida*. Boccaccio twice tells the story found in *The Franklin's Tale*: once in the *Decameron* and once in the *Filocolo*. Although the *Decameron* (1358) is now Boccaccio's best-known work, it was probably not known to Chaucer. *The Franklin's Tale* resembles the version of the story found in the *Filocolo*.

In Boccaccio's versions, the story has no connection with Brittany. It is not claimed that the story is a 'Breton Lay.' It was Chaucer who changed the location of the tale to Brittany. The Franklin's claim that his tale derived from a lay sung by the 'olde gentil Britouns' is a literary fiction.

The Canterbury Tales

In 1170 Thomas Becket, Archbishop of Canterbury, was murdered by followers of King Henry II. He soon came to be regarded as a martyr for the Christian faith. The site of his murder in Canterbury Cathedral was considered a particularly holy place, and attracted many pilgrims. In Chaucer's day it was the most popular place of pilgrimage in England.

In the Prologue to *The Canterbury Tales* Chaucer relates how he spent the night at the Tabard Inn at Southwark, near London, before setting out on such a pilgrimage. Some twenty-nine other pilgrims, bound on the same journey, were also staying at the inn, and Chaucer describes them all carefully. In the morning, all set off for Canterbury, accompanied by the host of the inn. The host proposed that, to amuse themselves on the journey, each pilgrim should tell two stories on the way to Canterbury, and another two on the way back to Southwark. Chaucer thus envisaged writing a collection of about one hundred and twenty stories. Had he completed his plan, *The Canterbury Tales* would have been the longest poem in the English language. In fact, he wrote only twenty-four tales, and not all of these are complete.

Each tale is not only a story in itself, but reflects the character and opinions of its teller. Some of the stories tell us a great deal about their tellers. They might be said to amplify the descriptions of the pilgrims given in the General Prologue to *The Canterbury Tales*. Furthermore, one pilgrim will take up a theme discussed by another, and give his own point of view on the subject. Again, some of the pilgrims quarrel, sometimes violently, with one another. They abuse each other, tell stories at one another's expense.

For example, the first pilgrim to tell a story is a Knight, a noble and dignified person. He tells a tale filled with high ideals and elevated philosophy. When he has finished, a drunken Miller insists on telling a story which he claims will 'quite' (balance, match) the Knight's Tale. He does indeed deal with the same subject—two young men in love with the same woman—but handles it in a far less elevated way than the Knight. In telling his story he offends a Reeve (a steward or overseer), who replies with an even coarser tale at the expense of the Miller.

Thus *The Canterbury Tales* is a series of discussions and arguments. It will be seen that *The Franklin's Tale* discusses subjects raised by previous speakers. It will also be seen that it reflects the Franklin's own ideals, attitudes and aspirations.

The Franklin

First, what was a Franklin? He was simply a landowner. He was a wealthy, but not aristocratic, member of society. In the General Prologue to *The Canterbury Tales*, Chaucer describes his Franklin as follows:

A FRANKELEYN was in his compaignye.
Whit was his berd as is the dayesye;
Of his complexioun he was sangwyn.

Wel loved he by the morwe a sop in wyn;
To lyven in delit was evere his wone,
For he was Epicurus owene sone,
That heeld opinioun that pleyn delit
Was verray felicitee parfit.
An housholdere, and that a greet, was he;
Seint Julian he was in his contree.
His breed, his ale, was alweys after oon;
A bettre envyned man was nowher noon.
Withoute bake mete was nevere his hous
Of fissh and flessh, and that so plentevous,
It snewed in his hous of mete and drynke,
Of alle deyntees that men koude thynke.
After the sondry sesons of the yeer,
So chaunged he his mete and his soper.
Ful many a fat partrich hadde he in muwe,
And many a breem and many a luce in stuwe.
Wo was his cook but if his sauce were
Poynaunt and sharp, and redy al his geere.
His table dormant in his halle alway
Stood redy covered al the longe day.
At sessiouns ther was he lord and sire;
Ful ofte tyme he was knyght of the shire.
An anlaas and a gipser al of silk
Heeng at his girdel, whit as morne milk.
A shirreve hadde he been, and a contour.
Was nowher swich a worthy vavasour.

(There was a Franklin in his company [that is, in the company of a Lawyer, who has just been described]. His beard was as white as a daisy. He was of a sanguine temperament. He loved a piece of bread dipped in wine in the morning. It was always his custom to live in delight, for he was a follower of Epicurus [the Greek philosopher] who believed that complete physical pleasure was perfect happiness. He kept up a great household; he was the Saint Julian of his country [Julian is the patron saint of hospitality]. His bread and his ale were always of the same quality. No man had a better stock of wine. His house was never without baked fish and meat, which was so abundant that it seemed to snow food and drink in his house, with every delicacy that one could imagine. He varied his food according to the seasons of the year. He had many a fat partridge in his coop, and many a bream and pike in his fishpond. Woe to his cook if his sauce were not pungent and sharp, and all his utensils ready. His fixed table always stood ready-laid in his hall, all day long. He presided as magistrate over the local courts; he was often the Member of Parliament. A knife and a silk purse, white as fresh milk, hung from his belt. He had been a sheriff and an auditor. There was nowhere such an impressive landowner.)

The student of *The Franklin's Tale* will find it very helpful to study this description carefully. It is not a very favourable one. The Franklin is a glutton, whose chief purpose in life is to gratify his appetites. He is hospitable, but his hospitality consists in inviting others to share his self-indulgence. He strives to impress other people with the lavishness of his entertainment. In attempting to imitate the splendour of an aristocratic household, he succeeds only in being vulgar, ostentatious and disgusting. These unpleasant aspects of his character will also be apparent in his tale, which is more concerned with the appearance than with the reality of nobility.

A note on the text

Chaucer wrote before the invention of printing. His works therefore circulated in manuscript form for the first hundred years of their existence. They were first printed by William Caxton in the fifteenth century. The best modern edition of *The Complete Works of Chaucer* is by F.N. Robinson (2nd. edition, Oxford University Press, London 1957. It is also published by Houghton Mifflin, New York). There are two good editions of *The Franklin's Tale* alone: by Phyllis Hodgson (Athlone Press, London, 1960) and A.C. Spearing (Cambridge University Press, Cambridge, 1966). Spearing's edition is highly recommended but it would be useful to consult Hodgson's also.

The three editions differ in their numbering of the lines. Spearing begins with the linking passage, 'the words of the Franklin to the Squire, and the words of the Host to the Franklin.' Hodgson begins with the Franklin's Prologue. The following table may be useful:

	SPEARING	HODGSON	ROBINSON
Linking passage:	1–36	[673–708]	673–708
Franklin's Prologue:	37–56	1–20	709–728
Franklin's Tale:	57–952	21–916	729–1624

For convenience Spearing's numbering is used in these notes but those of Hodgson (H) and Robinson (R) are given in parentheses. In quoting from the text Robinson's edition is used.

Part 2

Summaries
of THE FRANKLIN'S TALE

A general summary

The Franklin, having interrupted the Squire, is asked by the Host to tell a tale. He consents, saying that his tale will be a 'Breton Lay'. He asks pardon for his lack of learning; his tale must be told very simply.

In Brittany there was a knight who loved a lady. For long he wooed her until she agreed to marry him. He promised not to dominate her, but to obey her. The Franklin remarks that love can be based only on liberty and patience, not on domination. The knight, Arveragus, crossed the sea to England to win fame in tournaments, and remained there for two years.

His wife, Dorigen, was grieved at his absence. She was distraught when she saw the rocks along the sea-shore, fearing lest Arveragus's ship would be wrecked on them when he returned. To comfort Dorigen, her friends took her to dance in a garden. In the dance was a squire called Aurelius, who had loved Dorigen for two years, but had not dared to tell her. At last however he took courage and told her of his love. She replied that she would never deceive her husband, but playfully agreed to make love to him if he could remove all the rocks from the coast. Believing this to be impossible, Aurelius prayed frantically to his gods to perform this miracle, then collapsed in a faint. His brother carried him to bed, where he lay in torment.

Arveragus at last returned home, much to Dorigen's joy. Aurelius however lay for two years in bed. His brother, a scholar, remembered seeing a book of magic in Orleans and thought they might find a magician there who could remove the rocks. The two brothers set out for Orleans, and just outside the city met a magician who offered to remove the rocks for a thousand pounds. Augelius agreed to pay this sum, and the magician brought about a flood tide which made it appear that the rocks had vanished.

Aurelius visited Dorigen, pointed out that the rocks were gone, and asked that she keep her promise. She was horrified, and complained at length of her bad fortune. She considered killing herself, but at last told her husband the whole story. He told her that if she had given her promise to Aurelius, she should keep it. She must not, however, tell anyone what she had done.

Dorigen, weeping, went to keep her appointment. Aurelius met her, but seeing her grief and considering the honourable behaviour of her husband, released her from her promise. Dorigen returned to Arveragus, and the two lived happily ever after.

Aurelius, though he had not obtained what he wanted, still owed the magician a thousand pounds, an enormous sum of money. He took five hundred pounds and gave it to the magician, begging to be allowed time to obtain the rest. The magician was displeased that Aurelius could not pay promptly. He himself had kept his part of the bargain. He asked if Aurelius had not had his lady, as he had wished. Aurelius told his story, explaining how he had taken pity on Dorigen. The magician agreed to forgive Aurelius all his debt.

The Franklin concludes his tale by asking, 'Which of these characters was the most generous?'

Detailed summaries

The words of the Franklin to the Squire, and the words of the Host to the Franklin—Lines 1–36 (H [673–708], R 673–708)

The previous tale has been told by the Squire, a very long-winded young man. In over six hundred lines, the Squire has scarcely begun his story. The Franklin grows impatient and interrupts him, taking care to be very polite. 'Truly, Squire, you have acquitted yourself very well,' he says, 'considering your youth. You speak with much feeling, sir. I consider that there is nobody here who will be your equal in eloquence, if you survive.' He continues to praise the Squire, contrasting him with the Franklin's own son, who is worthless. The Host stops the Franklin, but is careful not to give the Squire opportunity to continue his long story. Instead, he seems to pretend that it is the Franklin who should be telling a story: 'You know well that each of you must tell at least a tale or two, or else break his promise.' The Franklin agrees to tell his story.

NOTES AND GLOSSARY

yquit: acquitted. In Middle English, y- is prefixed to past participles

gentilly: nobly. The Franklin greatly admires **gentillesse** (noble behaviour) which is indeed the theme of his tale

considerynge thy yowthe: note the Franklin's patronising manner. Actually the Squire has not performed very well at all

shal be:	note the future tense. The Squire is not *yet* very eloquent
vertu:	virtue, manliness
by the Trinitee:	by God
levere:	rather
swich:	such
been:	are
snybbed:	scolded
entende:	pay attention to
dees:	dice
despende:	waste
lese:	lose
usage:	custom
page:	servant
gentil wight:	noble person. *gentil, gentilly, gentillesse* are significant words for the Franklin, who would like to be thought *gentil* himself
pardee:	indeed
woost:	know
moot:	must
herkneth:	pay attention to
contrarien:	contradict, oppose

The Franklin's Prologue—Lines 37–56 (H 1–20, R 709–28)

In olden times, says the Franklin, the Bretons made lays about various happenings, which they either sung or read. He remembers one of them, and will do his best to tell it. He apologises however for his lack of skill in rhetoric. He is an unlearned man; he never read the Latin rhetorician Cicero. He knows nothing of rhetorical devices.

NOTES AND GLOSSARY

The Franklin claims that his tale is of Breton origin, and that he is ignorant of rhetoric, the art of literary composition. Both claims are false: his tale is taken from Boccaccio (see Introduction, p.9) and he is expert in rhetoric; this very passage is full of rhetorical devices.

hir:	their
diverse aventures:	various happenings
maden:	made; final -**n** sometimes indicates the plural form of a verb
redden:	read
oon:	one

hem: them
burel: unlearned
rude: rough
sleep: slept
Mount of Pernaso: Mount Parnassus, in Greece, home of the Muses, the goddesses of the arts
Marcus Tullius Scithero: Cicero (106–43BC) was a great Roman orator
colours: ornaments of rhetorical style
withouten drede: without doubt
swiche colours as growen in the mede: such colours as grow in the meadow (that is, flowers)
queynte: strange
My spirit feeleth noght of swich mateere: my spirit is unaffected by such things

---

The Franklin's Tale—Lines 57–88 (H 21–52, R 729–60)

In Brittany there was once a knight who loved a beautiful lady and served her for a long time. At last she took pity on him and accepted him for her husband. He swore never to exercise any mastery over her against her will, but rather to obey her in everything, except that he would be called the master for shame's sake. She in turn promised always to be true to him.

NOTES AND GLOSSARY
Armorik: *Armorica* was the ancient name for Brittany
dide his payne: took trouble
in his beste wise: as best he could
emprise: enterprise
wroghte: performed
er: before
oon the: one of the
therto: also
heigh kynrede: noble family
wel unnethes: scarcely
dorste: dared
obeysaunce: obedience
Hath swich a pitee caught of his penaunce: has taken such pity on his suffering
pryvely: secretly
fil of his accord: came to an agreement with him
han: have
maistrie: mastery, domination

Agayn:	against
kithe:	show
shal:	should
soveraynetee:	sovereignty, lordship
degree:	status
ful:	very
humblesse:	humility
profre:	propose
Ne wolde nevere God:	God forbid that ever
bitwixe:	between
tweyne:	two
As in my gilt:	through my fault
outher:	either
trouthe:	promise
breste:	break

Lines 89–130 (H 53–94, R 761–802)

The Franklin observes that friends must obey each other if they wish to stay together. Love cannot be forced: when domination comes, the God of Love flies away. Women and men desire to be free. Patience in love is a great virtue. Everyone does wrong sometime; one may not take revenge for every wrong. Therefore this wise knight has promised to be patient with his wife, and she has promised not to wrong him. This is a wise agreement; she has taken him both as her servant and as her lord. Having made this agreement, he takes her home and lives happily with her.

NOTES AND GLOSSARY

o:	one
saufly:	safely
everych oother:	each other
wol:	will
God of Love:	love is often personified in medieval literature as a winged god with bow and arrows to strike down his victims
of kynde:	by nature
thral:	slave
doon:	do
If I sooth seyen shal:	to tell the truth
at his advantage al above:	in a position of complete superiority
clerkes:	scholars, who would know the Latin proverb *vincit qui patitur*, 'he who is patient will conquer'

venquysseth:	conquers
seyn:	say
pleyne:	complain
Lerneth:	learn
so moot I goon:	I assure you
shul:	shall
wher so ye wole or noon:	whether you like it or not
ther no wight is:	there is nobody
dooth:	does
seith:	says
amys:	wrong
Ire:	anger
constellacioun:	the position of the stars (believed to affect men's behaviour)
chaungynge of complexioun:	change of bodily constitution
wreken:	avenged
lines 113–4:	'Anyone with any self-restraint will control himself as the situation demands'
suffrance hire bihight:	promised her to be patient
defaute:	fault
servage:	service
lordshipe above:	supreme rule
Sith:	since
certes:	certainly
acordeth:	agrees
Pedmark:	Penmarc'h, in Brittany
solas:	comfort, pleasure

Lines 131–68 (H 95–132, R 803–40)

Who but a married man could tell the joy that exists between husband and wife? This blissful life lasted a year and more, until this knight, Arveragus, went to England, to seek renown in arms, and stayed there two years. His wife, Dorigen, was greatly upset by his absence. Her friends did their best to comfort her, and managed to console her a little. Arveragus also wrote, promising to return home soon. She would otherwise have died of grief.

NOTES AND GLOSSARY

koude:	could
but:	unless
Kayrrud:	Kerru, in Brittany
cleped:	called

shoop:	arranged
eek:	also
Briteyne:	Britain—both Brittany and Great Britain were called *Briteyne*
lust:	desire
stynten of:	stop talking about
siketh:	sighs
whan hem liketh:	when it pleases them
line 147:	'She mourns, cannot sleep, wails, does not eat, complains'
destreyneth:	torments
sette at noght:	cared nothing for
hevy:	heavy, sorrowful
conforten:	comfort
in al that ever they may:	in every way they can
prechen:	exhort
causelees:	needlessly
sleeth:	is killing
cas:	case, situation
line 155:	'They do to her with all their diligence'
hire:	this word can mean both 'her' and 'their'
hevynesse:	sadness
By proces:	In course of time
everichoon:	everyone
graven:	engrave, carve
stoon:	stone
figure:	image
emprented:	imprinted
resoun:	reason
line 162:	'The imprint of their consolation'
thurgh:	through, because of
sorwe:	sorrow
aswage:	diminish
duren:	continue, persist
rage:	madness

Lines 169–84 (H 133–48, R 841–56)

Her friends, seeing her sorrow slacken, begged her to come and walk with them, to drive gloomy thoughts from her mind. She agreed to this. They took her to walk by the sea, but every time she saw a ship she complained, 'Alas! Is there no ship that will bring home my lord?'

NOTES AND GLOSSARY

slake:	slacken, abate
derke fantasye:	morbid imagination
saugh:	saw
faste by:	close to
an heigh:	high up
seigh:	saw
line 179:	'Sailing on their courses, wherever they wished to go'
line 184:	'Entirely cured of the pain of its bitter sorrow'

Lines 185–222 (H 149–86, R 857–94)

At other times she would sit thinking, and look down over the cliff; but when she saw the horrible black rocks, she was so frightened that she could not stand up. She would sit on the grass saying, 'God, you make nothing without reason. Why then have you made these rocks, which do no good, but only harm? Why have you made something which destroys so many men? May God protect my husband! I wish these rocks would sink into Hell!'

NOTES AND GLOSSARY

grisly:	horrible
verray:	real, true
adoun:	down
pitously:	pitiably
biholde:	look
sikes colde:	gloomy sighs
eterne:	everlasting
purveiaunce:	providence
governaunce:	control
In idel:	In vain, uselessly
feendly:	fiendish, diabolical
stable:	unchanging
line 200:	'Why have you made this unreasonable thing?'
ne:	nor
nys:	is not
yfostred:	benefited
bryd:	bird
to my wit:	as far as I can tell
anoyeth:	causes harm
al be they nat in mynde:	although they are not remembered
merk:	image (compare Genesis 1:26)

chiertee:	love
meenes:	means
as hem leste:	as it pleases them
line 215:	'Though I cannot discern the causes'
thilke = the ilke:	the same
as kepe:	may be protect
line 218:	'I leave all disputation to scholars'
sleen:	kill

Lines 223–52 (H 187–216, R 895–924)

Her friends saw that walking by the sea was only making matters worse, so instead they walked by rivers and springs and other pleasant places. They danced and played games. One morning—it was the sixth of May—they took her into a beautiful garden. They ate dinner, and then all except Dorigen began to dance and sing.

NOTES AND GLOSSARY

A beautiful garden is a very common feature in medieval literature. The most famous example is the Garden of Mirth in the thirteenth-century French poem *The Romance of the Rose* (c 1237), which Chaucer translated into English. Another such garden is described in Chaucer's *The Merchant's Tale*, which precedes *The Squire's Tale*. The garden, the month of May, and the dance are all closely associated with Love. When they are described, you may be sure a lover is about to appear.

disport:	recreation, amusement
shopen:	arranged
welles:	springs
delitables:	delightful
tables:	backgammon
morwe-tyde:	morning-time
maad:	made
ordinaunce:	arrangements
vitaille:	food
purveiaunce:	provisions
they goon and pleye hem: they go and amuse themselves	
sixte morwe:	sixth morning
curiously:	skilfully
prys:	worth
the verray paradys: the true Paradise, the garden of Eden	
to:	too

plesaunce:	delight
gonne:	began
moone:	moan, lament
lines 249–50	'Because she did not see him who was her husband and lord taking part in the dance'
nathelees:	nevertheless
slyde:	pass away

Lines 253–87 (H 217–51, R 925–59)

One of the men in this dance was a handsome young squire called Aurelius. He could sing and dance better than anyone. Moreover he was strong and virtuous and rich and wise, and held in great esteem by all. He had been in love with Dorigen for two years, but dared not tell her. He would hint at his love in his songs, saying how he loved in vain, and how he dared not tell his sorrow, but was suffering torment like a fiend in Hell; he would die, as Echo did for Narcissus. Sometimes he would look pleadingly at her at dances; but she knew nothing of what he meant.

NOTES AND GLOSSARY

The love-sick young man, pining with unrequited love, was a conventional figure in medieval literature. See Introduction (pp.7–9) for a discussion of Aurelius' malady. This description of Aurelius has similarities to Chaucer's portrait of the Squire, whose tale the Franklin has interrupted. Perhaps this description is intended as a compliment to the Squire, whom the Franklin evidently admires.

jolyer:	gayer
as to my doom:	in my opinion
passynge:	better than
sith:	since
discryve:	describe
beste farynge:	handsomest
on lyve:	alive
right:	very
prys:	esteem
sothe:	truth
unwityng:	without the knowledge
Venus:	goddess of love
ycleped:	called
aventure:	fortune
grevaunce:	distress

withouten coppe: without cup. What Chaucer means is uncertain; perhaps, 'Without measure'

penaunce: suffering

save: except that

wreye: reveal

layes, Songes, compleintes, roundels, virelayes: These are technical terms for various kinds of literary composition. *Lays* are narrative poems, such as *The Franklin's Tale* itself, but the term is probably used here more loosely, for any kind of song. *Complaints* are poems lamenting some grievance; Chaucer himself wrote several, including one to his purse, which was empty. *Roundels* and *Virelays* are both short poems with refrains, sometimes sung to accompany dances. These are all originally French literary forms

fury: In classical mythology, the three Furies tormented the damned in Hades. Chaucer however confuses them with the devils of Christian belief, who themselves suffer punishment as well as inflicting it

lines 279–80: The Latin poet Ovid tells how Echo, spurned by Narcissus, pined away until nothing remained of her but her voice

biwreye: betray, reveal

paraventure: perhaps

ther: where

kepen hir observaunces: perform their customs

entente: meaning

Lines 288–333 (H 252–97, R 960–1005)

Nevertheless it happened that, since they were old acquaintances, they fell into conversation. Seeing his opportunity, Aurelius at last revealed his feelings to Dorigen. She swore that she would never be untrue to her husband. However she said in jest that if he could remove all the rocks from the sea-coast, she would become his lover. She advised him to put such folly out of his mind, for what pleasure can a man take in loving the wife of another man, who can make love to her whenever he wishes?

NOTES AND GLOSSARY

Here, as several times in *The Franklin's Tale*, there is a difference between what the Franklin *says* is happening and what we ourselves *see* to be happening. This kind of *irony* is very common in Chaucer.

Thus, the Franklin has assured us that Aurelius dared not reveal his love, but was pining away in the conventional, expected, manner. However, on the first occasion we meet Aurelius he reveals his love to Dorigen readily enough, in a rather calculating fashion. Notice also Dorigen's habit of giving a 'final answer' and then qualifying it. See the discussions of Aurelius and Dorigen in Part 3.

worshipe:	reputation
yknowen hym:	made himself known, introduced himself
of tyme yoore:	long ago
drough:	drew
line 296:	'If I thought it would make your heart glad'
gerdon:	reward
brestyng:	breaking
reweth:	take pity
grave:	buried
leyser:	opportunity
do me deye:	cause me to die
gan:	began
erst:	before
yaf:	gave
knyt:	joined, meaning married
syn:	since
endelong Britayne:	from one end of Brittany to the other
That they ne lette:	so that they do not hinder
boot:	boat
ysene:	visible
trouthe:	promise, oath. Compare line 87. A solemn word
bityde:	happen
deyntee:	pleasure
whan so that hym liketh:	whenever it pleases him

Lines 334–72 (H 298–336, R 1006–44)

Aurelius was sad to hear this, and complained that it was impossible; he would die. Then her other friends came up, and the revels continued until sunset. All went home happy except for Aurelius, who seemed to feel the approach of death. He fell on his knees and prayed wildly, like one out of his wits, to Phoebus Apollo, the Greek sun-god.

NOTES AND GLOSSARY

siketh:	sighs
aleyes:	garden paths

line 342:	'And knew nothing of what had happened.' This line and lines 344–6 are an example of the rhetorical device *circumlocutio*. See Part 3, p.55
hewe:	hue, colour
th'orisonte:	the horizon
reft:	robbed of
asterte:	escape
him semed:	it seemed to him
gan holde:	held. *Gan* is an auxiliary verb used to form the past tense, like modern *did*
knowes:	knees
orisoun:	prayer
verray:	real
out of his wit he breyde:	he went out of his mind
nyste = ne wyste:	did not know
pleynt:	lament
the goddes:	the gods. Since the tale is set in the remote past, it is assumed that Aurelius worships the classical pagan gods, Apollo, Venus and so forth
Appollo:	Apollo, the sun-god
yevest:	give
after thy declinacioun:	according to your altitude. It was thought by medieval astrologers that the sun and the other heavenly bodies influenced affairs on earth by their position in the sky
herberwe:	lodging, position
Phebus:	Phoebus, another name for Apollo
merciable:	merciful
eighe:	eye
lorn:	lost, ruined
benignytee:	kindness
dedly:	dying
if yow lest:	if it pleases you
line 370:	'You can help me better than anyone except my lady'
voucheth sauf:	consent
devyse:	explain
holpen:	helped

Lines 373–414 (H 337–78, R 1045–86)

Aurelius prayed that Apollo would ask his sister Lucina, the moon-goddess, to cause a flood-tide to cover the rocks, so that he could tell

Dorigen that the rocks had vanished. Or if she would not do this, she must in her capacity as goddess of the underworld cause the rocks to sink into the ground. When he had finished his prayer, he fainted away, and his brother put him to bed.

NOTES AND GLOSSARY

This section is very complicated and difficult because Chaucer introduces so much astrological and mythological lore. Note again the ironic difference between what the Franklin *says* is happening and what we *see* happening. The Franklin says that Aurelius' prayer is mere raving, but actually Aurelius presumes to give his god precise directions as to how to help him. His prayer shows more cunning than madness. Note too that Aurelius' inclination is not to accept his lady's will, as did Yvain (see Introduction pp.8–9) but to manipulate her into making love to him. Such behaviour is not as *gentil* as the Franklin would have us suppose.

blisful:	blessed
Lucina:	another name for the moon-goddess Diana
sheene:	bright
Neptunus:	the sea-god Neptune
emperisse:	empress. She has power to overrule Neptune. Pagan mythology and medieval astrology are here combined with some genuine science: the moon really does influence the tides
quyked:	made alive
ful bisily:	very eagerly
moore and less:	great and small
do myn herte breste:	make my heart break
lines 385–6:	'On the next occasion when the sun will be in opposition to the moon (that is, at an angle of 180 degrees to it, a position which causes high tides), at which time the sun will be in the zodiac sign of Leo (a sign in which the sun's influence was thought to be particularly strong)'
lines 388–9:	'So that it rises at least five fathoms above the highest rock in Brittany'. A *fathom* is six feet, or about two metres
Holdeth youre heste:	keep your promise
line 397	'Then she will always be full'. A full moon causes high tides
spryng flood:	a 'spring' tide is a very high one

line 402:	'Into her own dark region'. Diana, under the name of Proserpina, was also goddess of the underworld
Pluto:	god of the underworld
mo:	more
Delphos:	Chaucer has confused *Delos* and *Delphi,* two shrines of Apollo in Greece
swowne:	swoon
penaunce:	suffering
line 414:	'As far as I am concerned, he may choose whether to live or die'

Lines 415–28 (H 379–92, R 1087–1100)

Meanwhile Arveragus had returned home. Dorigen was happy again. Averagus did not bother to ask her if anyone had spoken to her of love in his absence; he had no fears in the matter. He lived happily, dancing, jousting and entertaining his wife.

NOTES AND GLOSSARY

heele:	well-being
flour:	flower
line 422:	'In no way did he want to be suspicious'
line 425:	'He pays no attention to such matters'
justeth:	jousts
maketh hire good cheere:	entertains her

Lines 429–62 (H 393–426, R 1101–34)

For two years and more poor Aurelius lay in torment, unable to leave his bed. He told nobody except his brother about his affliction. At last his brother remembered that when he had been a student at Orleans, he had known someone with a book of magic spells, all about the different effects resulting from the various positions of the moon.

NOTES AND GLOSSARY

langour:	sickness
line 431:	'Before he could walk one foot on the ground'—that is, before he could get out of bed
clerk:	scholar
werk:	business
baar:	bore
Pamphilus and Galathee:	characters in a medieval love-story
ay:	always

arwe:	arrow. This refers to the idea that the God of Love shot an arrow into his victims' hearts (see the note on the God of Love, p.17)
kene:	sharp
sursanure:	a wound which has healed over on the surface, leaving the arrowhead inside. It is difficult to cure such a wound unless you can get the arrow out
weep:	wept
pryvely:	secretly
hym fil in remembraunce: he remembered	
been lykerous:	are eager
curious:	strange, occult
every halke and every herne: every nook and cranny	
Particuler:	unusual
say:	saw
magyk natureel:	*natural* magic, concerned with natural phenomena such as the movements of the planets, as opposed to *black* magic, concerned with evil spirits, which was strictly forbidden
felawe:	companion
Al:	although
ylaft:	left

Lines 463–98 (H 427–62, R 1135–70)

When he remembered this book, he was delighted, believing that his brother would soon be cured. He had heard how conjurers produced various illusions, and hoped that in Orleans he might find some old man who would make it appear that the rocks had vanished. Then Dorigen would have to keep her promise, or else be put to shame. He roused his brother and they set out for Orleans.

NOTES AND GLOSSARY

Anon:	immediately
warisshed:	cured
hastily:	quickly
siker:	sure
diverse apparences: various illusions	
subtile:	clever
tregetoures:	conjurers
lines 470–9:	such illusions were often performed as entertainment at feasts in Chaucer's time
wel:	certainly

line 474:	'Sometimes a grim lion has seemed to appear'
lym:	mortar
voyded:	dismissed, got rid of
line 479:	note the insistence on 'seemed': the conjurers produce unreal illusions
above:	also
han:	have
yvoyded:	removed
everichon:	every one
brynke:	shore
wowke:	week
line 491:	'Then she will have to keep her promise, or he will at least put her to shame.' The moral degeneracy of this plan should not be overlooked. In a genuine aristocratic romance no hero would think of manipulating his lady in this way, and certainly would not contemplate publicly shaming her
lenger:	longer
Unto:	To
comen is:	has come
confort:	encouragement
stirte:	rose
forthward is he fare:	he has set forth
lissed:	relieved

Lines 499–536 (H 463–500, R 1171–1208)

When they were within a short distance of Orleans, they met a young scholar who greeted them in Latin, who already knew why they had come. This magician took them home and entertained them well. Before they went to supper he showed them forests and parks full of wild deer being hunted. When the deer were gone he saw falconers hawking and knights jousting. Then he saw his lady in a dance in which he himself took part, or so it seemed. And when the magician saw it was time, he clapped his hands and the illusions vanished. And yet they had never left his house, but had been in his study all the time.

NOTES AND GLOSSARY

a two furlong or thre:	two or three furlongs away. A furlong is about two hundred metres
line 502:	'Who greeted them politely in Latin.' Latin was the common language of scholars
wonder:	wonderful

dawes:	days
lighte:	got down
Hem lakked:	they lacked
vitaille:	food
er:	before
hertes:	harts, male deer
hye:	high
ye:	eye
fauconers:	falconers, men who hunt birds with hawks
ryver:	riverbank
dide hym swich plesaunce: gave him such delight	
as hym thoughte:	as it seemed to him
maister:	master, expert
ago:	gone
wight:	person

Lines 537–83 (H 501–47, R 1209–55)

They went in to supper, and afterwards discussed how much the magician would charge to remove all the rocks of Brittany. He insisted on being paid a thousand pounds. Aurelius readily agreed, saying that he would give the whole world, if he owned it, in return for Dorigen. They went to bed, and in the morning Aurelius took the magician home with him. It was now December, and the sun was in the sign of Capricorn; the weather was wet and cold.

NOTES AND GLOSSARY

sith:	since
whan it liketh yow: whenever you wish	
as for the beste:	that's the best thing to do
tretee:	negotiation
gerdon:	reward
Gerounde, Saine:	the French rivers Gironde and Seine are about the same distance from Brittany, on either side
make it straunge:	drove a hard bargain
Lasse:	less
line 553:	'Nor would he willingly act for that much'
which that men seye is round: people in Chaucer's time were well aware that the world was round	
yeve:	give
line 558:	'This bargain is completed, for we are in agreement'
line 559:	Notice the solemn promise, very like Dorigen's, which Aurelius gives to the magician

tarie:	delay
my feith to borwe:	my word as a pledge. Another solemn promise
line 564:	Aurelius sleeps almost all night—the first good night's sleep he has had for years
of penaunce hadde a lisse:	had relief from suffering
righte:	direct
line 570:	'And got down where they were to stay.' That is, they rode directly home, not stopping until they reached Aurelius' house
remembre:	remind
lines 573–83:	This passage is a long rhetorical elaboration of the simple statement that it was December
Phebus:	the sun
wax:	grew
hewed:	coloured
laton:	brass
declynacion:	altitude
burned:	burnished
yerd:	garden
Janus:	The god of the turn of the year, who gives his name to January. He is depicted with two faces (hence 'double berd'), one looking back at the old year and the other looking forward to the new
bugle horn:	drinking-horn
stant:	stands
brawen:	meat
tusked swyn:	the wild boar, a kind of pig with tusks
Nowel:	an exclamation of joy, sung at Christmas

Lines 584–624 (H 548–88, R 1256–96)

Aurelius showed great respect to the magician, begging him to cure his malady as quickly as possible. The magician took pity on him and, after some very complicated astrological calculations, brought about such a high tide that it seemed as if all the rocks had disappeared.

NOTES AND GLOSSARY

Again, this passage is difficult because the Franklin shows off his knowledge of abstruse astrological terms. Chaucer evidently enjoyed making poetry out of catalogues of scientific terms; there are several such passages in his works. Note that the magician does not really remove the rocks; he creates an illusion, making it seem that they have disappeared. The Franklin himself is much concerned with making an impression, of projecting an image of courtliness and gentility. The student should not be worried if he cannot understand every detail of this section. The astrological terms are of a very specialised nature, and their precise significance is disputed by experts. A detailed explanation of a passage such as this would not normally be expected in a school or college examination.

dooth chiere and reverence: entertains and shows respect
doon his diligence: make every effort
line 588: 'Or he would pierce his own heart with a sword'
routhe: pity
he spedde him that he kan: he made as much haste as possible
waiten: watch out for. The magician must wait until the stars and planets are in the right positions
conclusion: experiment, operation
apparence: illusion
jogelrye: conjuring
line 594: 'I do not know any astrological terms.' This, like the Franklin's claim to be ignorant of Rhetoric (lines 44–56) is obviously untrue; the passage which follows is full of astrological terms. The line is an example of the rhetorical device *diminutio*. See discussion of Rhetoric in Part 3 (pp.54–8)
wene: think
japes: tricks
tables Tolletanes: Toledan tables, that is, astrological tables invented by scholars from Toledo, in Spain. These were in wide use in Chaucer's time
corrected: tables devised for the longtitude of Toledo would need to be adjusted for use in Brittany
collect, expans yeeris, rootes: In astrological tables, the *root* is the first date for which figures stating the positions of the planets are given. Often the *root* is the date of the Birth of Christ. Tables for *collect* years showed the adjustments to be made to the figures given for the *root* year to allow for the passage of large periods of time, such as hundreds of years. A table of *expans* years showed the adjustments necessary for shorter periods. By using the tables for *collect* years and *expans* years together, the astronomer could infer the positions of the heavenly bodies in the year he required
geeris: equipment

as been:	such as
centris:	centres of the orbits in which the planets move
argumentz:	figures from which certain astronomical calculations can be made

proporcioneles convenientz: tables for determing the positions of the planets during periods of less than a year

equacions:	small adjustments
eighte speere:	It was believed that the universe consisted of nine concentric spheres. At the centre was the Earth. In the first sphere was the Moon, then in order Mercury, Venus, the Sun, Mars, Jupiter and Saturn. The eighth sphere contained the stars, and the ninth was the *primum mobile* or 'first mover' which imparted motion to the other spheres. The signs of the Zodiac were considered to be divisions of the ninth sphere. Originally they had coincided with constellations in the eighth sphere. However, the eighth sphere was slowly rotating, so the signs of the Zodiac no longer coincided exactly with the constellations from which they took their names. Alnath is a star in the constellation of Aries, the Ram; it had moved away from the sign of Aries in the sphere above, that is, the ninth sphere; the magician skilfully calculated exactly how far it had moved
mansioun:	position of the moon; see line 458
weel:	well
face, terme:	divisions of the signs of the Zodiac
everydeel:	everything
Acordaunt:	according
meschaunces:	accursed customs
hethen:	heathen
useden:	practised
thilke:	those
a wyke or tweye:	a week or two

Lines 625–66 (H 589–630, R 1297–1338)

Aurelius waited anxiously for the result of this experiment, and when he saw the rocks had disappeared, he fell on his knees and thanked the magician. Then he made his way to the temple, where he knew he would find Dorigen, and said to her: 'My true lady, whom I most fear and love, were I not so sick with love for you that I must soon die at your feet, I would not tell you of my sorrow. Yet remember what you promised, and do not break your word. I have done as you commanded: the rocks have disappeared.'

NOTES AND GLOSSARY

wher:	whether
line 634:	'and he has made his way straight to the temple'
dredful:	fearful
cheere:	behaviour, manner
salewed:	saluted
righte:	true
nere it:	were it not
disese:	sickness
dyen:	die
line 644:	' I would tell you nothing of how sorrowful I am'
certes:	certainly
outher:	either
pleyne:	complain
sle:	kill
giltelees:	innocent
verray:	real, true
aviseth yow:	consider
woot:	know
hight:	promised
lines 651–2:	'Not that I claim anything from you, my sovereign lady, of right, but through your mercy.' This is hypocrisy. Aurelius is using the courtly manner and language of an Yvain (see Introduction p.9) but in a very uncourtly spirit. He is blackmailing Dorigen
yond:	yonder
bihighten:	promised
youre trouthe plighten ye:	you made a promise
al be that:	although
lines 659–60:	note again the hypocrisy of Aurelius's claim. His main concern at this point is certainly not Dorigen's honour
do:	done
vouche sauf:	agree
biheste:	promise
quyk or deed:	alive or dead
line 665:	'It rests entirely with you whether you kill me or let me live'

Lines 667–706 (H 631–70, R 1339–78)

Aurelius took his leave, and Dorigen stood astonished; all the blood drained from her face. She thought she had never been caught in such a trap. She went home and lamented this strange event. She could not tell anyone about it, for Arveragus was out of town, but she complained as follows: 'Alas, Fortune, you have entrapped me. There is no escape: I must suffer either death or dishonour. And there are many old stories which shows that it is better to die than to be dishonoured. When the Thirty Tyrants killed Phidon at Athens, they had his daughters brought in, stripped naked, and made them dance in their father's blood. These woeful maidens, rather than lose their virginity, jumped secretly into a well and drowned themselves.

NOTES AND GLOSSARY

nas = ne was:	was not
wende:	thought
monstre:	unnatural thing
merveille:	marvel, miracle
unnethe:	scarcely
swowneth:	swoons
cheere:	appearance
line 683:	Here begins a long complaint against Fortune, which in the Middle Ages was often personified as a goddess. In a tradition deriving from the Roman author Boethius (AD 480–524) she was imagined as turning a huge wheel, to which men were chained (hence 'cheyne' in line 684). They were carried to the top of the wheel—that is, to the height of worldly success—but then, as the wheel continued to turn, plunged down again to the bottom. The lament or complaint was a common set-piece in medieval rhetoric. A complaint could be a poem in its own right. Chaucer wrote several such complaints: a *Complaint unto Pity*, a *Complaint to his Lady*, *The Complaint of Mars*, *The Complaint of Venus*, and even a *Complaint to his Purse*
unwar:	unawares
t':	to
socour:	help
bihoveth me:	is necessary for me
chese:	choose
nathelees:.	nevertheless

have I levere:	I would rather
lese:	lose
quyt:	set free
ywis:	truly
doon trespas:	commit sin
line 695:	Here Dorigen begins to adduce stories, all taken from the *Adversus Jovinianum*, a very popular book in the Middle Ages, written by St Jerome (AD 342–420). The ostensible purpose of these illustrative stories or *exempla* is to confirm Dorigen in her resolve to die rather than to suffer dishonour; however, they serve rather to delay her action. She does not in the event kill herself, and the effect of her lament is therefore anti-climax. Dorigen does not live up to the heroic examples of olden days. The first story concerns an incident which took place in 404BC, when the Thirty Tyrants seized power in Athens
beren:	bear
thritty:	thirty
cursednesse:	wickedness
atte:	at the
doghtres:	daughters
t'areste:	to arrest
biforn hem:	before them
in despit:	cruelly
hir:	their
fadres:	father's
God yeve hem meschaunce!:	God give them misfortune
maydenhede:	virginity
line 705:	'They secretly jumped into a well and drowned themselves, as the book says.' The idea of maidens jumping *secretly* into a well is rather ludicrous, and perhaps prepares us to take the lament less seriously than Dorigen would wish

Lines 707–46 (H 671–710, R 1379–1418)

Dorigen continues her lament: 'The people of Messene sent for fifty virgins of Sparta whom they intended to rape. But every one of them chose to die rather than to lose her virginity. Why should I then be afraid to die? Consider also the tyrant Aristoclides who loved a virgin called Stymphalides. When her father was murdered, she went to the temple and clung to the statue of Diana, and would not let go until she herself was killed. If virgins behaved like this, a wife should certainly kill herself rather than be defiled. Hasdrubal's wife also killed herself rather than suffer shame; and Lucretia, after being raped, killed herself. The seven virgins of Miletus acted similarly. I could tell more than a thousand stories on this theme. Abradates' wife killed herself, saying, "At least nobody will defile my body, if I can help it." '

NOTES AND GLOSSARY

leete enquere and seke: had enquiry and search made

Lacedomye:	Sparta
eke:	also
hir:	their
nas = ne was:	was not
entente:	will
Chees:	Chose

been oppressed of hir maydenhede: have their virginity violated

line 714:	Chaucer has a remarkable technique of forming doubts in his readers' minds by raising questions which are either not answered, or are answered in an unsatisfactory way. Here Dorigen asks why she should not kill herself. It may not perhaps have occurred to the reader that she *should* kill herself; but once the question has been raised, it is undeniable that within the terms of the ethic Dorigen professes to admire, the right thing *would* indeed be to kill herself. She does not
Aristoclides:	tyrant of Orchomenos in Arcadia
heet:	called
Dianes temple:	Diana was the goddess of chastity
hente:	took
arace:	tear away
selve:	same
sith:	since
despit:	disdain
thinketh me:	seems to me
birafte hirself:	deprived herself of
skipte:	jumped
vileynye:	shame
Milesie:	Miletus, in Asia Minor (modern Turkey) was destroyed by the Gauls in 276BC
mo:	more

touchynge:	concerning
Hirselven slow:	Killed herself
glyde:	flow

Lines 747–84 (H 711–48, R 1419–56)

Dorigen continues, 'Why should I relate more *exempla*, since so many have killed themselves rather than be violated? I conclude that it is better for me to kill myself than to be defiled. I will be true to Arveragus, or else kill myself, as did Demotion's daughter. O Scedasus, it is very sad to read how your daughters died; it is even sadder how the Theban virgin killed herself because of Nicanor. Another Theban virgin killed herself because a Macedonian had raped her. What shall I say of Nicerates' wife, who killed herself for the same reason? Alcibiades' mistress chose rather to die than to leave his body unburied. What does Homer say of Penelope? All Greece knows of her chastity. Laodomya would not live after the death of Protesilaus, nor Portia after the death of Brutus. The perfect wifehood of Artemisia is honoured far and wide. Queen Teuta, your wifely chastity is an example to all wives. I could say the same of Bilia, of Rhodogune and of Valeria.'

NOTES AND GLOSSARY

lines 747–51:	again, Dorigen by concluding that it is best to kill herself draws attention to the fact that she is not committing suicide
line 752:	Dorigen, having decided not to relate any more examples, proceeds to do so, thus delaying any action still further
Demociones doghter:	the virgin daughter of Demotion, on hearing of the death of her fiancé, killed herself lest she should be compelled to marry someone else
Cedasus:	Scedasus of Boeotia, whose daughters, after being raped, killed each other for shame
for swich a maner cas:	for just such a reason
wel:	even
Nichanore:	Nicanor, one of Alexander the Great's officers
Macidonye:	Macedonia, north of Greece
redressed:	avenged
Nicerates:	was killed by the Thirty Tyrants of Athens and his wife killed herself rather than become their victim
birafte hirself hir lyf:	took her own life
Alcestis:	the daughter of Peleas and Anaxibia died in place of her husband Admetus

Alcibiades:	the celebrated Athenian statesman and general was also murdered by the Thirty Tyrants, and his mistress Timandra buried his body in defiance of their orders. A brave action, but with little relevance to Dorigen's situation
Omer:	Homer, who in the *Odyssey* tells of Penelope's faithfulness to Odysseus
pardee:	indeed
Laodomya:	when Protesilaus was killed at Troy, his wife Laodamia accompanied him to Hades
Porcia:	Portia, wife of Brutus, who killed herself, fearing for her husband's life
line 778:	'To whom she had entirely given her heart'
parfit:	perfect
Arthemesie:	Artemisia built a great monument to her husband Mausolus. Again, there is no relevance to Dorigen's situation
thurgh:	through
Barbarie:	barbarian lands
Teuta:	was not married. To cite her as an example of wifely chastity is therefore entirely beside the point!
Bilyea:	Bilia tolerated her husband's bad breath. Again, this is not Dorigen's problem
Rodogone:	Rhodogune killed her nurse, who had tried to persuade her to remarry
Valeria:	refused to take a second husband

Lines 785–826 (H 749–90, R 1457–98)

Dorigen lamented in this way for a day or two, always intending to kill herself. However, Arveragus came home on the third night and asked why she was crying. She told him the whole story. He listened without showing sorrow or anger, and told her that if she had given a solemn promise, she should keep it. At this point however he burst into tears, and made her promise never to tell anyone what had happened; he would do his best to endure his sorrow. Then he called two servants, and told them to take Dorigen to the place where she was to meet Aurelius; but they were not told the purpose of her journey.

The Franklin remarks that perhaps some of his hearers will think Arveragus a fool to have put his wife in such peril; he asks us to be patient and hear the end before we judge.

NOTES AND GLOSSARY

This section calls for very careful study. The Franklin clearly admires the nobility of Arveragus in making his wife keep her promise. We need not necessarily agree with him. His remark that some of us may think Arveragus a fool is very typical of Chaucer's technique. He raises a problem which may not have occurred to us and then, instead of resolving it, gives an unsatisfactory answer which only serves to draw more attention to the problem. Thus, the Franklin suggests that some of us may think Arveragus a fool for putting his wife in such peril. Instead of showing that Arveragus's behaviour was wise, he merely hints that the tale will have a happy ending. This may be so, but it does not make Arveragus's behaviour any less foolish. He was not to know that Aurelius would take pity on Dorigen.

Notice, too, that Arveragus's concern is for *himself*, not for Dorigen. His worry is that people will get to hear of the affair. He wishes to protect his image, just as in agreeing to let Dorigen have her will in everything he nevertheless reserved to himself the *name* of lord, for shame's sake (lines 79–80). In all this Arveragus reflects the Franklin's concern with splendid outward appearances, the form if not the substance of aristocratic behaviour. Arveragus undertakes to endure his own sorrow as best he can (line 812) but gives no thought to *Dorigen's* feelings. In other words he has abdicated his responsibility as a husband. He is indeed a lord in name only. One may wonder if their agreement is such a 'humble, wise accord' as the Franklin supposes (line 119).

line 786:	observe the irony of this line
thridde:	third
weep:	was weeping
line 790:	'And she went on weeping all the more'
devyse:	tell
Is ther oght elles?	Is there anything else? A phrase commonly used by priests hearing confessions
God helpe me so as wys!:	may God help me indeed!
lat slepen that is stille:	compare the modern proverb, 'Let sleeping dogs lie.' This is evidently the motto of Arveragus, who, like the Franklin, loves above all 'to live in ease' (line 116). It is a curious reaction to the situation, which might be thought to require action
paraventure:	perhaps
line 802:	'You shall keep your promise, by my faith'
so wisly:	indeed
levere:	rather
ystiked:	stabbed

verray: true
brast anon to wepe: immediately burst into tears
up: on
contenance of hevynesse: appearance of sorrow
demen: judge
cleped: called
hir: their
ne wiste: did not know
thider: there
line 820: 'He would tell nobody what he intended'
line 821: 'Perhaps many of you, truly'
lewed: stupid
jupartie: peril
upon hire crie: condemn *her*. Notice how the Franklin, having cast doubts on *Arveragus's* behaviour, immediately shifts his attention to Dorigen without really answering the question he has raised
yow semeth: appears to you
demeth: judge

Lines 827–72 (H 791–836, R 1499–1544)

Aurelius happened to meet Dorigen on her way to the garden where she had promised to meet him. He asked her where she was going. 'To the garden,' she said, 'as my husband told me, to keep my promise, alas!' Aurelius wondered at this, and took pity on her in her misery, and on Arveragus who had told her to keep her promise. He decided to do without what he wanted, rather than perform such a wicked deed. He said 'Madam, tell your lord Arveragus that since I see his noble behaviour towards you, and since I also see your great distress, and that he would rather suffer shame than that you should break your promise to me, I prefer to suffer woe than to harm the love between you. I release you from your promise. I give you my word, I shall never reproach you about any promise. And now I take my leave; you are the truest and best wife I ever met.' Every wife, though, should beware of making a promise like Dorigen's. Thus a squire can do as noble a deed as a knight can.

NOTES AND GLOSSARY
highte: was called
of aventure: by chance
happed: happened
Amydde: in the middle of

quykkest:	busiest
bown:	prepared
forth right:	directly
to the gardyn-ward:	on his way to the garden
maner:	sort of
of aventure or grace:	by chance or providence
saleweth:	greets
glad entente:	good will
whiderward she wente:	where she was going
gan wondren:	wondered, marvelled
cas:	situation
line 847:	'He was so unwilling that his wife should break her promise'
caughte of this greet routhe:	was moved to pity by this
lust:	desire
abide:	abstain
heigh:	great
cherlissh:	villainous
wrecchednesse:	wickedness
Agayns:	Contrary to
franchise:	generosity
gentillesse:	noble behaviour
seyth:	say
departe:	split, divide
relesse:	release
hond:	hand
quyt:	discharged
serement:	oath
maad:	made
heerbiforn:	before now
sith:	since
thilke:	that
lines 869–72:	since quotation-marks were not in use in Chaucer's day, it is not clear whether these lines are part of Aurelius' speech, or a comment by the Franklin
withouten drede:	without doubt

Lines 873–912 (H 837–76, R 1545–84)

She thanked him on her bare knees, and went home to her husband and told him all that had happened. You may be sure he was pleased to hear it. Why make a long story of it? Arveragus and Dorigen lived happily ever after. But Aurelius, who had wasted his money, cursed the day that he was born. 'Alas,' he said, 'that I ever promised the magician a thousand pounds. What shall I do? I will have to sell my patrimony and be a beggar. I shall go to the magician and ask him for time to pay.' He took five hundred pounds to the magician and asked for time to pay the remainder, saying, 'Sir, I have never yet failed to keep my promise. Truly, my debt to you will be paid, whatever becomes of me, even if I have to go begging in my bare shirt. But if you would agree, upon security, to allow me two or three years to pay, all will be well; if not, I must sell my patrimony.'

NOTES AND GLOSSARY

is she fare:	she has gone
siker:	sure
apayd:	pleased
endyte:	write
line 880:	'Pass their life in supreme happiness'
eft:	afterwards
al forlorn:	completely lost
bihighte:	promised
pured:	refined
wighte:	weight
philosophre:	this word is often used in Middle English to mean an adept in occult sciences, such as alchemy or astrology. Translate 'magician' or 'astrologer'
namoore:	no more
fordo:	undone
moot I nedes:	I will have to
but:	unless
assaye:	try
cofre:	chest
avaunt:	boast
sikerly:	surely
quyt:	paid
kirtle:	tunic, shirt
seuretee:	security
respiten:	grant respite to

Lines 913–52 (H 877–916, R 1585–1624)

This astrologer gravely replied, 'Have I not kept my agreement with you?' 'Yes, indeed,' said Aurelius. 'Have you not enjoyed your lady?'

asked the astrologer. 'No,' said Aurelius, sighing. 'Why not?' asked the astrologer. Aurelius told him his story, how Arveragus had preferred to die of sorrow than let his wife break her word; how sorry Dorigen had been, and how unwilling she was to be a wicked wife, and how she would rather have died. She had given her word in all innocence; she had never before even heard of illusions. Aurelius concluded, 'This made me take pity on her, and as generously as he sent her to me, so I sent her back to him. That's all there is to it; there's no more to say.'

The astrologer answered, 'Dear brother, each of you acted nobly towards the other. You are a squire and he is a knight, but God forbid that a scholar should not be able to perform a noble deed as well as either of you! Sir, I forgive you the thousand pounds, as if you had just now sprung from the ground and had never met me before. I will not take a penny from you for my labour; you have paid me well for my food. Goodbye!' And he took his horse and rode away.

The Franklin concludes his tale by asking, 'Sirs, which of them do you think was the most generous? Tell me before you go any further. I know no more; my story is at an end.'

NOTES AND GLOSSARY

thee liketh:	pleases you
siketh:	sighs
line 922:	'There is no need to tell you it again.' Nevertheless the Franklin does recapitulate what had happened. The nobility of Arveragus and Dorigen grows a little in the process; there has been no suggestion before now that Arveragus was likely to die of his grief; and Dorigen had had ample opportunity if she really preferred death to dishonour
erst:	before
frely:	generously
this al and som:	that's the long and the short of it
leeve:	dear
everich:	each
for his blisful might:	in his blessed power
koude:	could
it is no drede:	without doubt
cropen:	sprung up
travaille:	labour
vitaille:	food
ynogh:	enough
Lordynges:	Sirs
fre:	generous

Part 3

Commentary

The purpose of *The Franklin's Tale*

It is useful to distinguish between Chaucer's purpose in writing *The Franklin's Tale* and the Franklin's purpose in telling his tale.

Chaucer's purpose in writing *The Canterbury Tales* is to delight his readers. He does this more fully by telling tales which are not only entertaining in themselves, but also reflect the character and interests of the tellers. The tellers, as well as the tales, are of course the creations of Chaucer. It is often said that he creates a little world, a miniature model of the society of his time. Certainly, the group of pilgrims represents a fairly wide spectrum of fourteenth-century society. A religious pilgrimage would have been the only occasion on which such a varied group could come together.

The characters tell their tales in accordance with the suggestion of the Host, as a means of passing the time more pleasantly. The pilgrim whose tale receives most favour will receive a supper at the expense of the others. The Franklin, more than any of the others, wishes to eat that supper. Eating supper is the greatest pleasure in his life, as is seen from his description in the General Prologue to *The Canterbury Tales*. In order to receive the supper he must win the votes of his fellow-pilgrims. His purpose in telling his tale is therefore to please as many of his companions as possible. In particular he strives to please the influential members of the party.

The most influential character on the pilgrimage is a Knight. Now the Franklin is called upon to tell his tale immediately after he has interrupted the Squire. The Squire is the Knight's son. There is a danger that both will have been offended by the interruption. The Franklin takes immediate steps to prevent any such reaction. Consider his remarks about the virtue of Patience, and particularly lines 107–114: 'For in this world, certainly, there is no person who does not do or say something wrong at some time. Anger, sickness, the position of the stars, wine, grief or changes in bodily constitution often cause people to do or say something wrong. A man may not be revenged for every wrong. Anyone with any self-restraint will control himself as the situation demands.'

This passage has little to do with the situation between Arveragus and Dorigen, but much to do with the situation between the Franklin and the Knight. The Franklin in effect asks the Knight to be patient, not to take revenge for a slight insult. He goes on to tell a tale in which the leading characters are a Knight and a Squire, portrayed in what the Franklin believes to be a flattering manner.

Another pilgrim who carries a lot of weight is the Wife of Bath. This amiable lady has been married five times, and is looking for a sixth husband. She has very definite ideas about how a marriage should be conducted. She believes that the woman should be the boss, or, as she puts it, have the *soveraynetee* or *maistrie*. She tells a tale in which a knight agrees to grant his wife the *maistrie*, and as a result enjoys a happy life. The Franklin has Arveragus grant Dorigen the *maistrie* at the beginning of his tale, and she agrees to be true to him in words very like those of the Wife of Bath.

Another major character is the Clerk, or Scholar. He has told a story about the virtue of Patience. Note that the Franklin pays him a compliment: 'Patience is a great virtue, certainly, for it overcomes, as these *clerks* say, in things where rigour never could succeed' (lines 101–3). Furthermore, another character in *The Franklin's Tale* is the *clerk* of Orleans, whose behaviour is said to be as noble as that of the knight or the squire.

The Clerk's Tale had been followed by that of the Merchant. *The Merchant's Tale*, like *The Franklin's Tale*, concerns a knight who marries a woman who is in turn loved by a squire. A garden, similar to the one described in *The Romance of the Rose*, plays a prominent part in the story. The Franklin may therefore be sure that the Merchant will be interested in his subject-matter. Certain of the Franklin's lines are very like lines in *The Merchant's Tale*:

> Who koude telle, but he hadde wedded be,
> The joye, the ese, and the prosperitee
> That is bitwixe an housbonde and his wyf?
> A yeer and moore lasted this blisful lyf . . .
>
> (131–4)

Line 134, with its suggestion that married bliss does not last, perhaps suggests that the Franklin shares the Merchant's cynical view of marriage.

So the Franklin knows how to please and flatter as many as possible of his companions, how to express opinions which he knows will find favour with them. We should remember that he has often been a Member of Parliament. It is always difficult to please everybody, and the Canterbury pilgrims are a varied assortment of people, holding widely differing views. In trying to agree with them all, the Franklin perhaps lays himself open to the charge of being 'two-faced', that is, a hypocrite. Thus, Arveragus abandons his claim to *maistrie*, but a few lines later insists on retaining

> ... the name of soveraynetee,
> That wolde he have for shame of his degree.
>
> (79–80)

Arveragus is to be both master and servant:

> Heere may men seen an humble, wys accord;
> Thus hath she take hir servant and hir lord,—
> Servant in love, and lord in mariage.
> Thanne was he bothe in lordship and servage.
>
> (119–22)

Aurelius claims to love his lady above all things, and yet tries to manipulate her into committing a humiliating act of adultery. Arveragus promises never to exercise *maistrie* over Dorigen, yet orders her to keep her appointment with Aurelius and forbids her, on pain of death, ever to mention the affair. Dorigen vows to kill herself rather than be untrue to her husband, yet a few lines later she sets off to keep her appointment. The characters in the tale, like the teller, are constantly in two minds. Notice that Janus, the two-faced god, is described in the middle of the tale:

> Janus sit by the fyr, with double berd,
> And drynketh of his bugle horn the wyn;
> Biforn hym stant brawen of the tusked swyn,
> And 'Nowel!' crieth every lusty man.
>
> (580–3)

Surely Janus stands for the Franklin himself, who is not only two-faced, but loves to sit by the fire drinking wine and eating roast pork. Janus is, as it were, the deity presiding over this curiously ambivalent tale.

Irony in *The Franklin's Tale*

Irony is the expression of one's meaning by means of language which seems to convey the opposite, or a different, meaning. Thus if the weather is bad, and we say 'Lovely weather, isn't it?' we are speaking ironically.

A kind of irony of which Chaucer is very fond is to speak through the mouth of a narrator, for example the Franklin. Chaucer may put into the mouth of such a narrator statements with which he himself would not agree, and which he does not intend his readers to believe.

Thus, the Franklin may assure us that Arveragus was a wise and worthy knight, that his marriage with Dorigen was a secure and happy one, that Dorigen preferred death to dishonour. We are at liberty to agree or disagree with these opinions. The judgement is left to the reader. And the judgement will be based on what the reader sees happening, not on the Franklin's comments on the action. There may be an ironic difference between what the Franklin says is happening and what the reader sees to be happening.

Sometimes the difference is so striking that the reader is forced to exercise his critical faculties, to disagree sharply with the Franklin. The reader must therefore be very active. He cannot simply listen to the Franklin telling his tale, but must participate in the tale as a critical observer. Chaucer invites his readers to take such a role when he has the Franklin say:

> Paraventure an heep of yow, ywis,
> Wol holden hym a lewed man in this
> That he wol putte his wyf in jupartie.
> Harkneth the tale er ye upon her crie.
> She may have bettre fortune than yow semeth;
> And whan that ye han herd the tale, demeth. (821–6)

(See the notes to this passage in the Summary, pp. 39–41)

The characters

This ironic technique is essential to Chaucer's portrayal of character. We cannot rely solely on what the Franklin tells us about a person; we must compare this carefully with what we see the person *do*. We may find a considerable ironic difference. Let us examine the three main characters in *The Franklin's Tale*—Arveragus, Dorigen and Aurelius—and compare what the Franklin says about them with what we see of their personalities revealed in their actions.

The student may wish to perform this exercise for himself before comparing his conclusions with the remarks below.

Arveragus

The Franklin's opinion of Arveragus is entirely favourable. Dorigen, he says, is attracted by the knight's *worthynesse* (line 66). This does not mean much however; almost all Chaucer's characters, even the rascals, are described as *worthy*. Being *worthy*, for Chaucer, means being an outstanding example of whatever it is you are. A *worthy* knight therefore is simply a knightly knight.

Dorigen is particularly attracted by his *meke obeysaunce*, his meek submissiveness (line 67). The student will remember from the Introduction to these *Notes* (pp.8–9) how Yvain amazed his beloved by his meek submissiveness to her will. Such behaviour on the part of a lover is conventional in medieval literature.

Dorigen also remarks on his *gentillesse*, his nobility (line 82). This is a key word, for the whole tale is an essay on what the Franklin considers to be *gentillesse*. Since however the Franklin is not himself *gentil*, but observes *gentillesse* from the outside, he sees its external features rather than its inner spirit.

The Franklin calls Arveragus this *wise, worthy knyght* (line 115). Again this does not advance matters much. The Franklin had already said that Arveragus was *worthy*; now he says he was *wise*. Being *wise* for Chaucer is not so much a matter of being intellectually accomplished as being experienced and competent at whatever it is you do. So to call a man a *wise, worthy knyght* is no more than to call him a knightly knight, good at being a knight.

The next thing the Franklin tells us about Arveragus is that he is *of chivalrie the flour* (line 416). *Chivalrie* is simply another word for the quality of knightliness, so we now learn that Arveragus, a knightly knight good at being a knight, is the flower of knightliness. He appears to be a singularly one-dimensional character.

He is called *The fresshe knyght, the worthy man of armes* (line 420). Since a knight is by definition a man of arms and we know already that he was *worthy*, this line tells us only that he was *fresshe*. This is a rather general adjective, meaning 'fresh, eager, bold, vigorous, bright,' used regularly of knights in Middle English romances.

When Arveragus next appears he is called *this worthy knyght* (line 788) and again at line 845 he is *the worthy knyght*, which we know already; finally at line 855 he is credited with *grete gentillesse*.

All that the Franklin says about Arveragus therefore amounts to this: he is, in the Franklin's opinion, all that a knight should be. Let us see if his behaviour justifies the Franklin's opinion.

The first thing Arveragus does in the tale is to woo Dorigen. He scarcely dares tell her his 'woe, pain and distress' (line 65). These symptoms of love are conventional enough, and can be compared with those of Arcite in *The Knight's Tale*. In agreeing to obey her in everything he is again behaving conventionally, *As any lovere to his lady shal* (line 78). Note that the motive for his indulgence is *To lyve in ese* (line 116). He likes a quiet life, without complications: *Thus been they bothe in quiete and in reste* (line 88). He does not wish to know if anyone has spoken to Dorigen of love in his absence:

No thyng list hym to been ymaginatyf,
If any wight hadde spoke, whil he was out,
To hire of love; he hadde of it no doute.
He noght entendeth to no swich mateere,
But daunceth, justeth, maketh hire good cheere ...
(422–6)

When confronted with Dorigen's problem, he tells her, rather unhelpfully:

... lat slepen that is stille.
it may be wel, paraventure, yet to day.   (800–1)

He hopes that if he ignores the problem, it will go away. He prefers to bear a grief than to do anything about it: *As I may best, I wol my wo endure* (line 812). He is in short a morally lazy person, like the Franklin himself.

We may question his behaviour in leaving his wife to go to England,

To seke in armes worshipe and honour;
For al his lust he sette in swich labour;
And dwelled there two yeer, the book seith thus.
(139–41)

'The book says so.' It is remarkable how often when one of his characters does something questionable, Chaucer insists that his source says so, that he is not responsible for his character's action. It is selfish to leave one's wife alone for two years while one is enjoying oneself. As it happens, Arveragus's absence causes Dorigen great distress and is ultimately responsible for her predicament. It is true that it is conventional behaviour, in medieval romances, for the husband to leave his wife for long periods in order to *seken in armes worshipe and honour*. However, this action is also conventionally the cause of much distress. Thus, in the story of Yvain, the hero leaves his wife for a year to engage in jousting. When he does not return at the agreed time his wife, a more independent person than Dorigen, sends a message telling him never to return. Yvain, thus rejected, goes mad.

Arveragus's selfishness is seen too in his remark to Dorigen, *As I may best, I wol my wo endure* (line 812). He is concerned with his own sorrow, not with Dorigen's feelings. His main worry is lest anyone else should hear of the affair. He wishes to keep up appearances.

Finally, we should not let pass unchallenged his assertion that *Trouthe is the hyeste thyng that man may kepe* (line 807). It was a well-established moral principle, in the Christian ethics of Chaucer's day, that one is under no obligation to keep a promise to do something evil: two wrongs do not make a right. But perhaps it is unreasonable to expect Arveragus, who knows only such morality *as hethen folk useden in thilke dayes*, to act according to medieval Christian ethical principles.

Dorigen

The Franklin tells us very little about Dorigen except that she was beautiful and of noble parentage (lines 62–3). Aurelius thinks she is

> ... the treweste and the beste wyf
> That evere yet I knew in al my lyf.   (867–8)

Aurelius however is in love with her and is therefore hardly a reliable witness. We must observe her behaviour, and draw our conclusions accordingly.

The first time we see Dorigen, she is being gradually won over by Arveragus: *But atte laste she ... fil of his accord* (lines 66, 69). This is typical of her behaviour throughout the tale. She begins by giving a firm *No*, which is softened by persuasion to a reluctant and conditional *Yes*. Thus, she is persuaded to stop grieving and go for a walk with her friends. The process is well described in the image of a stone being gradually chipped away by the sculptor's mallet:

> By process, as ye knowen everichoon,
> Men may so longe graven in a stoon
> Til som figure therinne emprented be.
> So longe han they conforted hire, til she
> Receyved hath, by hope and by resoun,
> The emprentyng of hire consolacioun,
> Thurgh which hir grete sorwe gan aswage;
> She may nat alwey duren in swich rage.
>
> (157–64)

Every time we see Dorigen, she is in the process of changing her mind. She strikes resolute poses, but cannot remain resolute for long. Thus she gives Aurelius a final answer:

> I wol been his to whom that I am knyt.
> Taak this for fynal answere as of me.
>
> (314–15)

Unfortunately however she cannot leave matters quite so final:

> But after that in pley thus seyde she:
> 'Aurelie' quod she, 'by heighe God above,
> Yet wolde I graunte yow to been your love,
> Syn I yow se so pitously complayne ...
>
> (316–19)

A final answer should be final. Dorigen's afterthought perhaps shows a little insensitivity to Aurelius's feelings. It was not the moment to speak *in pley*.

The most remarkable insight into Dorigen's character comes in her long soliloquy (lines 670–784) in which she determines to die rather than suffer dishonour. She cites example after example from antiquity to show that death is the only honourable course. It soon becomes apparent, however, that these examples serve, not to spur Dorigen on to action, but to delay action altogether. Dorigen's examples become less and less relevant to the matter in hand. She is simply substituting words for action.

There is even a suggestion in the tale that Dorigen's grief is not real, but an act put on to conform to the rules of conventional behaviour:

> For his absence wepeth she and siketh,
> As doon thise noble wyves whan hem liketh.
>
> (145–6)

'She weeps and sighs for his absence, as these noble wives do *when it pleases them*'—as if they had any choice in the matter, as if the feelings of noble ladies were not real but a matter of pretence and of keeping up appearances. This perhaps tells us something about how the Franklin sees *gentillesse*, as a matter of external observances rather than of inner qualities.

Aurelius

The Franklin tries to portray Aurelius as a conventional young man in love. But with Aurelius, more so than with the other two characters, the Franklin fails to penetrate the surface of convention. Aurelius goes through the external actions thought proper to a lover in medieval romance. Thus, like Arcite in *The Knight's Tale*, he lies in bed for two years and more, suffering torment because of his love.

His manner of speech is conventional. In his complaint to Dorigen (lines 295–306), almost every word and expression could be paralleled in other romances. The last seven lines of this speech are so full of amatory clichés—conventional expressions—as to be almost a parody of medieval love-poetry:

> For wel I woot my servyce is in vayn;
> My gerdon is but brestyng of myn herte.
> Madame, reweth upon my peynes smerte;
> For with a word ye may me sleen or save.
> Here at youre feet God wolde that I were grave!
> I ne have as now no leyser moore to seye:
> Have mercy, sweete, or ye wol do me deye!
>
> (300–6)

There is however a vital difference between Aurelius and the conventional lover of medieval romance. This will be seen if we compare his complaint with a thoroughly conventional little poem of Chaucer's called *A Complaint to his Lady*. This may be taken as highly typical of the love-poetry of the time. Here is the last stanza:

> But I, my lyf and deeth, to yow obeye,
> And with right buxom herte hooly I preye,
> As is your moste plesure, so doth by me;
> Wel lever is me liken yow and deye
> Than for to anythyng or thynke or seye
> That yow myghte offende in any tyme.
> And therfor, swete, rewe on my peynes smerte,
> And of your grace graunteth me som drope;
> For elles may me laste no blis ne hope,
> Ne dwelle within my trouble careful herte.

The language is very similar (note particularly *rewe on my peynes smerte*) but here we find an element of *submissiveness* not found in Aurelius's speech. Chaucer allows the lady to do what she likes with him; he would rather die than cause her distress. Likewise Yvain (see Introduction) is willing to suffer death at his lady's hands, if that is what she wants. Aurelius is far more aggressive. Rather than die, he is all too willing to cause his lady distress. He manipulates her into a position where she must either break her word or become his mistress.

If we needed a single word to describe Aurelius, it would be *calculating*. Conventional lovers lose their wits; Aurelius keeps his wits about him. Though the Franklin is at pains to assure us that 'For verray wo out of his wit he breyde' (line 355) and 'He nyste what he spak' (line 356), Aurelius manages to give Phoebus Apollo a lecture, containing detailed and complicated instructions as to how to help him.

His speech to Dorigen (lines 639–66) asking her to keep her word, deserves careful study. Again, it is full of amatory clichés: 'And lothest were of al this world displese,' 'I for yow have swich disese,' 'I moste dyen heere at youre foot anon,' 'Ye sle me gilteless for verray peyne' and so on.

The whole speech, however, is thoroughly hypocritical. Aurelius claims to be acting in the most polite and correct way. He appeals not to her pity, but to her honour; he claims nothing of right, but asks for her grace; he confesses his own unworthiness. He even claims, in a crowning piece of hypocrisy, to be more concerned with her honour than with his own feelings:

Madame, I speke it for the honour of yow
Moore than to save myn hertes lyf right now ... (659–60)

He puts the moral onus on Dorigen, again and again reminding her that she has given her *trouthe*: 'Avyseth yow er that ye breke youre trouthe,' 'Ye woot right wel what ye bihighten me,' 'Wel ye woot what ye han hight,' 'God woot, ye seyde so,' 'Have youre biheste in mynde.' Under cover of conventional courtly language he is forcing her to act against her will rather than submitting humbly to her will, *As any lovere to his lady shal.*

Rhetoric

Rhetoric was a part of the basic course of studies in medieval schools. The trivium or elementary course consisted of three subjects: *grammar*, the study of the Latin language; *rhetoric*, the art of literary composition, whether of poetry, letters or sermons; and *dialectic*, that is, logic.

From the twelfth century onwards the rules of rhetoric were widely used, not only in Latin compositions, but in the vernacular languages. Most medieval writers show some acquaintance with rhetorical techniques.

Medieval rhetoric sought to *embellish* a story, to *amplify* it by various devices known as *colours* or *figures*. A previous narrator, the Clerk or Scholar of Oxford University, had been expert in rhetoric, and the Host had asked him not to use his tale as an occasion to display his expertise:

Youre terms, youre colours, and youre figures,
Keepe hem in stoor til so be that ye endite
Heigh style, as whan that men to kynges write.
Speketh so pleyn at this tyme, we yow preye,
That we may understonde what ye seye.

The Franklin however denies any knowledge of rhetoric:

> I lerned nevere rethorik, certeyn;
> Thyng that I speke, it moot be bare and pleyn.
>
> (47–8)

But this very denial is an example of the rhetorical figure *diminutio*, whereby one modestly disclaims any poetic ability in order to gain the sympathy of one's audience. Notice also that in the course of this *diminutio*, the Franklin makes exactly the same point several times, in different words. Thus, after claiming not to have learned rhetoric, he goes on:

> I sleep nevere on the Mount of Pernaso (49)

—He has not slept on Mount Parnassus, where he might have gained an acquaintance with the Muses, the patron gods of poetry and the other arts; in other words, he has not learned the art of rhetoric. He continues:

> Ne learned Marcus Tullius Scithero (50)

—He has not read Cicero, the great rhetorician. Furthermore:

> Colours ne knowe I none, withouten drede (51)

—He does not know about rhetorical *colours*. And so he goes on. This repetition of an idea in different words is itself a rhetorical colour, called *expolitio*. Furthermore, to talk about 'sleeping on Mount Parnassus' or 'reading Marcus Tullius Cicero' is a roundabout way of saying that he knows no rhetoric. To convey an idea in this roundabout way is yet another rhetorical figure called *circumlocutio*. Also, the idea of 'sleeping on Mount Parnassus' is borrowed from the classical Latin poet Persius.

So the Franklin, while claiming to be ignorant, is revealing a knowledge of Latin poetry. He does so again in the next two lines:

> But swiche colours as growen in the mede,
> Or elles swiche as men dye or peynte
>
> (53–4)

The comparison between rhetorical *colours* and the colours of flowers is found frequently in learned medieval Latin poetry, and the comparison between the poetic art and that of painting is found in the *Ars Poetica* of the classical Latin writer Horace.

Thus the Franklin, in the process of claiming ignorance, is giving an impressive display of rhetorical figures and classical learning. The display is rather overdone, rather ostentatious, and this reflects the Franklin's own character.

Despite the Franklin's disclaimer, there is abundant use of rhetorical figures in his tale. Lines 89–114, beginning 'For o thyng, sires, saufly dar I seye,' in which the Franklin turns aside from his narrative to discuss the virtue of Patience, is an example of the figure *diversio*, that is, digression. This *diversio* contains within itself several other rhetorical figures. Consider lines 101–3:

> Patience is an heigh vertu, certeyn,
> For it venquysseth, as thise clerkes seyn,
> Thynges that rigour sholde nevere atteyne.

These lines form a *sententia*, a moral generalisation arising out of the narrative, a figure much recommended by the rhetorical textbooks. Notice also the use of *expolitio* in the passage: the point made in lines 107–8 is repeated in different words in lines 109–11, and the point made in line 112 is repeated in different words in lines 113–14:

> For in this world, certein, ther no wight is
> That he ne dooth or seith somtyme amys.
> Ire, siknesse, or constellacioun,
> Wyn, wo, or chaungynge of complexioun
> Causeth ful ofte to doon amys or speken.
> On every wrong a man may nat be wreken.
> After the tyme moste be temperaunce
> To every wight that kan on governaunce.   (107–14)

Aurelius's first speech to Dorigen is again constructed according to the rules of rhetoric:

> 'Madame,' quod he, 'by God that this world made,
> So that I wiste it myghte youre herte glade,
> I wolde that day that youre Arveragus
> Wente over the see, that I, Aurelius,
> Hadde went ther nevere I sholde have come agayn.
> For wel I woot my servyce is in vayn;
> My gerdon is but brestyng of myn herte.
> Madame, reweth upon my peynes smerte;
> For with a word ye may me sleen or save.
> Heere at youre feet God wolde that I were grave!
> I ne have as now no leyser moore to seye;
> Have mercy, sweete, or ye wol do me deye!'
> (295–306)

The first five lines here are an example of the figure *circuitio*: that is, they do not state Aurelius's business directly, but hint at it. Actually, Aurelius does not say directly anywhere in the passage that he loves Dorigen, so the whole speech could be regarded as a *circuitio*. Again, there are instances of *expolitio*: the point of lines 295–9 is repeated briefly in line 304; line 301 repeats the idea of line 300, and lines 302–3 are recapitulated in line 306.

Aurelius's second speech to Dorigen (lines 639–66) has a more elaborate structure. Here the rhetoric serves an ironic purpose. Although the language is polite and the rhetoric is correct and dignified, Aurelius's meaning is far from correct. There is thus a jarring contrast between form and content.

Aurelius several times uses the device of *expolitio* in this speech. Having made the point that he is in danger of death (*I moste dyen heere at youre foot anon*) at line 643, he repeats it in different words at lines 645 (*outher moste I dye or pleyne*), 646 (*Ye sle me giltelees*), 647 (*But of my deeth ...*), 650 (*Er ye me sleen*), 660 (*to save myn hertes lyf*), 664 (*quyk or deed*), and 665 (*to do me lyve or deye*). Likewise Dorigen's promise is alluded to several times in different terms. The figure *praecisio* (breaking off suddenly, leaving a sentence unfinished) is used several times in the passage. Aurelius uses the figure *transgressio*, that is, the inversion of natural word-order, to express his reluctance to trouble Dorigen:

Nere it that I for yow have swich disese
That I moste dyen heere at youre foot anon,
Noght wolde I telle how me is wo bigon.

(642–4)

There is a digression or *diversio* at lines 652–3 and again at line 658. Lines 659–60 are a *contentio* or antithesis, and the last four lines of the speech are a *conclusio* or summary. And many other rhetorical figures are used in this carefully-constructed speech.

We could mention many other passages which are constructed according to the rules of rhetoric, such as Aurelius's complaint to the gods (lines 359–407) or Dorigen's long lament (lines 683–784). Let us be content however to note one last example:

But sodeynly bigonne revel newe,
Til that the brighte sonne loste his hewe;
For th'orisonte hath refte the sonne his lyght,—
This is as much to seye as it was nyght!

(343–6)

Here lines 343 and 344 are a *circumlocutio* for the statement that it was night, as the Franklin acknowledges playfully in line 346. The acknowledgement however shows how self-conscious the Franklin's use of rhetoric is: he is showing off his cleverness. This is typical of the Franklin's ostentatious character. Or, to put it another way, Chaucer characterises the Franklin by means of the rhetoric he puts into his mouth.

Some significant themes

Love and marriage

Love was an important theme in medieval literature. There is a certain conventional mode of behaviour to which most lovers in medieval literature conform. Typically, the man suffers agonies through his love for the lady, and only with difficulty does he find the courage to tell her about his condition. Thus it is said of Arveragus,

> That wel unnethes dorste this knyght, for drede,
> Telle hire his wo, his peyne, and his distresse.
>
> (64–5)

Similarly Aurelius had loved Dorigen for two years and more,

> But nevere dorste he tellen hire his grevaunce.
> Withouten coppe he dranke al his penaunce.
>
> (269–70)

The lover is said to 'serve' his lady; that is, he performs feats of arms or other tasks in her honour. *The Franklin's Tale* begins:

> In Armorik, that called is Britayne,
> Ther was a knyght that loved and dide his payne
> To *serve* a lady in his beste wise;
> And many a labour, many a greet emprise
> He for his lady wroghte, er she were wonne.
>
> (57–61)

Likewise Aurelius composes 'layes,/Songes, compleintes, roundels, virelayes' in his lady's honour (lines 275–6). He seems to think that this activity constitutes 'service', for he says ' . . . wel I woot my servyce is in vayn' (line 300).

Usually the lover's 'service' is rewarded when his lady accepts him as her husband. Thus at the end of *The Knight's Tale*, Emily marries Palamon and they live happily ever after. Many medieval romances, however, take as their theme the difficulties that arise in married life. In the tale of *Yvain* by Chretien de Troyes (see Introduction pp.8–9) the lovers marry early in the story and the rest of the plot has to do with a crisis which arises in their married relationship. This is also true of the plot of *The Franklin's Tale*. It is also true of two other stories in *The Canterbury Tales*, those of the Clerk and the Merchant. The Wife of Bath too has much to say about the tribulations of married life.

Some scholars have considered therefore that the prologues and tales of the Wife of Bath, the Clerk, the Merchant and the Franklin constitute a 'Discussion of Marriage'. According to these scholars, the Wife of Bath opens the debate with the suggestion that the woman should be the dominant partner—that is, she should have the 'soveraynetee' or 'maistrye'. The Clerk then tells a tale in which the woman is humble and obedient to her cruel husband. The Merchant holds a very cynical view of marriage, and tells a sarcastic tale in which an unpleasant young woman deceives her even more unpleasant husband. The Franklin, according to these scholars, concludes the debate by offering a picture of the ideal marriage, in which each partner obeys the other and does not insist on having the 'maistrye'.

There is undoubtedly some truth in this theory, and the student may wish to read the other three tales to decide for himself to what extent they constitute a 'Discussion of Marriage'. Certainly, various aspects of the problem of 'maistrye' in marriage are discussed in the course of the four tales. However, many other things are also discussed. It is perhaps arbitrary to isolate marriage as a theme uniting them.

The four tales do not form a continuous sequence; they do not even occur in the same order in all manuscripts of *The Canterbury Tales*. The tales of the Friar and the Summoner intervene between those of the Wife of Bath and the Clerk, and that of the Squire comes between those of the Merchant and the Franklin. So if there is a 'Discussion of Marriage' it suffers much interruption.

Furthermore, other tales also discuss the trials of married life. We could enlarge the 'Discussion of Marriage' to include most of the tales, in which case the idea would serve little critical purpose. Marriage is, after all, one of the most common of human activities, and it is not very remarkable that many of Chaucer's tales mention it.

Also, the idea of a 'Discussion of Marriage' should not distract us from the fact that *The Franklin's Tale* is not *about* marriage. It is about *Gentillesse, Trouthe* and *Fredom*, as understood by the Franklin. Likewise *The Clerk's Tale* is not *about* marriage; it is about the virtue of Patience, as understood by the Clerk.

Finally, the 'Discussion of Marriage' theory supposes that the Franklin closes the debate by portraying an 'ideal' marriage. The student must ask himself if the marriage of Arveragus and Dorigen is indeed ideal. Is it not rather disastrous? This is a matter of opinion, and as has often been said in these *Notes*, the student need not assume that the Franklin's opinion is the 'correct' one. Each reader must make up his own mind.

Adultery

Although many medieval love-stories regard marriage as the natural end of love, there are also many in which adulterous love—that is, love between a man and another man's wife—is tolerated. There are many medieval versions of the story of Lancelot, who is in love with Guinevere, wife of the legendary King Arthur. Another popular story of the time was that of Tristan and Iseult, in which the love is again adulterous. Some of the Breton Lays of Marie de France (see Introduction pp.6–7) deal with adulterous love.

Aurelius is thus acting in a conventional enough manner when he declares his love for a married woman. However there is a contrast between the highly conventional language with which he declares his love to Dorigen (lines 295–306; see Summary of these lines, pp.23–4 and also the discussion of Rhetoric above, pp.54–8) and the very realistic, down-to-earth language in which she replies:

'Is this youre wyl,' quod she, 'and sey ye thus?
Nevere erst,' quod she, 'ne wiste I what ye mente.
But now, Aurelie, I knowe youre entente,
By thilke God that yaf me soule and lyf,
Ne shal I nevere been untrewe wyf
In word ne werk, as fer as I have wit;
I wol been his to whom that I am knyt.
Taak this for fynal answere as of me.'

(308–15)

There is no trace here of the formal and conventional 'language of love' which Aurelius uses. Aurelius's love is shown up as a sordid and rather childish passion.

Unfortunately, Dorigen allows herself to lapse into the 'language of love' when she speaks 'in pley':

Yet wolde I graunte yow to been youre love,
Syn I yow se so pitously complayne.

(318–19)

This playful, conventional language is the cause of her future problem. She cuts it short, however, and sends Aurelius away with some very realistic language:

> Lat swiche folies out of youre herte slyde.
> What deyntee sholde a man han in his lyf
> For to go love another mannes wyf,
> That hath hir body whan so that hym liketh?   (330–3)

Trouthe

Trouthe means a solemn promise, or in a more abstract sense 'honesty' or 'fidelity'. Many medieval stories concern the difficulty of trying to keep a solemn promise which has been given rashly or in jest. The plot of *Sir Gawain and the Green Knight*, a poem written by a contemporary of Chaucer, centres on a promise by Gawain to allow the Green Knight to cut off his head.

Trouthe, as a virtue, was considered particularly appropriate to knights. Thus Chaucer's Knight is said in the Prologue to *The Canterbury Tales* to love '*Trouthe* and honour, fredom and curteisie.' Arveragus, the knight of *The Franklin's Tale*, considers that 'Trouthe is the hyeste thyng that man may kepe' (line 807).

Notice how many solemn promises are made in the tale. First Arveragus makes a promise to Dorigen:

> Of his free wyl he swoor hire as a knyght
> That nevere in al his lyf he, day ne nyght,
> Ne sholde upon hym take no maistrie
> Agayn hir wyl, ne kithe hire jalousie,
> But hire obeye, and folwe hir wyl in al.   (73–7)

Next Dorigen makes a promise to Arveragus:

> Sire, I wol be youre humble trewe wyf;
> Have heer my trouthe, til that myn herte breste.
>   (87–8)

Then Dorigen makes her unfortunate promise to Aurelius. Though she is speaking 'in pley' she gives him her *trouthe*:

> I seye, whan ye han maad the coost so clene
> Of rokkes that ther nys no stoon ysene,
> Thanne wol I love yow best of any man,
> Have heer my trouthe, in al that evere I kan.
>   (323–6)

Aurelius certainly insists that Dorigen's jesting words did constitute a promise. He tells her, 'Avyseth yow er that ye breke youre *trouthe*' (line 648), and reminds her that 'wel ye woot what ye han *hight* ' (line 651) and 'Ye woot right wel what ye *bihighten* me' (line 655) and 'in myn hand youre *trouthe* plighten ye/To love me best' (lines 656–7). In releasing Dorigen from her promise, he uses legal language such as was used in referring to solemn contractual obligations:

> I yow relesse, madame, into youre hond
> Quyt every serement and every bond
> That ye han maad to me as heerbiforn,
> Sith thilke tyme which that ye were born.
> My trouthe I plighte, I shal yow nevere repreve
> Of no biheste . . .
>
> (861–6)

Likewise Aurelius gives a solemn promise to the magician: 'Ye shal be payed trewely, by my *trouthe*' (line 559). And the magician in turn gives his word to Aurelius: 'have heer my feith to borwe' (line 562). Aurelius takes his promise seriously: 'My *trouthe* wol I kepe, I wol nat lye' (line 898). And he tells the magician, 'I failled nevere of my *trouthe* as yit' (line 905). The magician asks, 'Have I nat holden covenant unto thee?' (line 915) and he releases Aurelius from his promise in the same exaggerated terms as Aurelius had used in releasing Dorigen:

> Sire, I releesse thee thy thousand pound,
> As thou right now were cropen out of the ground,
> Ne nevere er now ne haddest knowen me.
>
> (941–3)

There is thus a series of solemn promises binding the various characters together: Arveragus and Dorigen; Dorigen and Aurelius; Aurelius and the magician. The problem arises when one promise conflicts with another. Dorigen has given her *trouthe* to Arveragus to be his 'humble, trewe wyf'. This oath implies that she will be faithful to him, not taking any other man as a lover. In keeping her *trouthe* to Aurelius, she is thus breaking her previous, and far more solemn, *trouthe* to Arveragus. Similarly Arveragus has sworn to Dorigen never to exercise dominion over her against her will. Yet this is exactly what he does, in making Dorigen, much against her will, keep her *trouthe* to Aurelius. Arveragus and Dorigen can keep one promise only by breaking others. 'Trouthe is the hyeste thyng that man may kepe' is a fine principle, but very difficult to put into practice.

Fredom

Fredom means 'generosity, liberality'. Again, it is a virtue considered particularly appropriate to knights. The Knight on the Canterbury pilgrimage loves 'Trouthe and honour, *fredom* and curteisie.' It is clearly a virtue much admired by the Franklin, for he is renowned for his hospitality, and hospitality is closely related to generosity. It is the *fredom* of Arveragus, Aurelius and the magician which the Franklin admires. Aurelius says:

> . . . right as *frely* as he sente hire me,
> As *frely* sente I hire to hym ageyn.   (932–3)

And the Franklin concludes his tale by asking, 'Which was the mooste fre, as thynketh yow?' (line 950). He means 'Who was the most generous?' However, *fre* can also mean 'free'. It is in fact the same word; the spelling varies in Middle English. *Fredom* also means simply 'freedom', and the tale is also about freedom, or the lack of it. It is appropriate that the Franklin should take an interest in freedom, for a franklin is simply a *free*holder, one who owns his own land without having to pay rent to someone else.

The Franklin announces his theme early in his tale:

> Love is a thyng as any spirit *free*.
> Wommen, of kynde, desiren libertee,
> And nat to been constreyned as a thral;
> And so doon men, if I sooth seyen shal.   (95–8)

Despite the Franklin's insistence that love cannot be constrained, Aurelius tries to force Dorigen to love him. He manipulates her into a position where she must either yield to him or be shamed. Dorigen is aware of being trapped, of being no longer free to act as she wishes:

> 'Allas,' quod she, 'on the, Fortune, I pleyne,
> That unwar wrapped hast me in thy cheyne,
> Fro which t'escape woot I no socour . . .'
>
> (683–5)

Dorigen's husband sends her, much against her will, to keep her appointment with Aurelius; Aurelius sends her back again. To use the word *frely* of sending her is ironic, for clearly she is anything but a free agent. One answer to the question, 'Which was the mooste fre?' would be 'Certainly not Dorigen!' Despite her husband's promise she does what she is told to do by others.

Gentillesse

Gentillesse is nobility, the behaviour appropriate to noble people. The Franklin admires this quality, and is disappointed that his own son is not associating with *gentil* people and learning *gentillesse* from them. He says to the Squire, whom he regards as a model of *gentillesse*,

> . . . he hath levere talken with a page
> Than to comune with any *gentil* wight
> Where he myghte lerne gentillesse aright.   (20–2)

In his tale the Franklin relates a series of actions which he regards as examples of *gentillesse*. Aurelius refrains from committing an act 'Agayns franchise and alle *gentillesse*' (line 852). He responds to Arveragus's 'grete *gentillesse*' (line 856). And the Franklin comments,

> Thus kan a squier doon a *gentil* dede
> As wel as kan a knyght, withouten drede.   (871–2)

Aurelius takes five hundred pounds to the magician,

> And hym bisecheth, of his *gentillesse*
> To graunte hym dayes of the remenaunt.   (902–3)

In explaining the situation to the magician, he refers again to Arveragus's *gentillesse*; and the magician sums up,

> . . . Leeve brother,
> Everich of yow dide *gentilly* til oother.
> Thou art a squier, and he is a knyght;
> But God forbede, for his blisful myght,
> But if a clerk koude doon a *gentil* dede
> As wel as any of yow, it is no drede!   (935–40)

The Franklin establishes therefore that a squire or a scholar can perform a *gentil* deed as well as a knight. But why should anyone have doubted this? Simply because in the Middle Ages *gentillesse* implied not only noble behaviour, but noble—that is, aristocratic—birth. The Franklin is not himself of *gentil* birth, but wants to be thought capable of *gentillesse*. He is anxious that his son should learn *gentillesse*. He wants to demonstrate that he is not disqualified by birth from so doing. The point of his tale therefore is that any man, regardless of his position in life, can perform a *gentil* deed.

The Franklin is not the only one on the pilgrimage to hold this opinion. The Wife of Bath had maintained it with some vigour in her tale:

For gentillesse nys but renomee
Of thyne auncestres, for hire heigh bountee,
Which is a strange thyng to thy persone.
Thy gentillesse cometh from God allone.
Thanne comth oure verray gentillesse of grace;
It was no thyng biquethe us with oure place.

(*Gentillesse*, noble birth, is only the renown of your ancestors, because of their goodness. It has nothing to do with you personally. Your own *gentillesse* comes from God alone. So our true *gentillesse* is a gift from God; it is not bequeathed to us along with our position in life.)

The Wife had quoted a number of ancient authors in support of her opinion. The Franklin would not therefore have been thought revolutionary in holding it. He might however have been criticised on the grounds that his understanding of *gentillesse* was somewhat deficient. He sees it as consisting of outward appearances rather than any inner spirit. So his hero Arveragus does not mind giving up the reality of *maistrie* in marriage provided that he can retain the outward appearance, 'the *name* of soveraynetee.' His chief concern at Dorigen's predicament seems to be that other people might hear of it. She is to keep up appearances,

Ne make no contenance of hevynesse,
That folk of yow may demen harm or gesse.   (813–14)

Aurelius also is less than truly *gentil*. His release of Dorigen is admirable, but his behaviour up to this point had been contemptible. The magician likewise performs a *gentil* deed in forgiving Aurelius his debt, but up to this point had been willing to accept a large sum of money in return for using his magic to bring distress and shame to an innocent woman. And Dorigen falls short of the example set by the noble women of ancient times. After calling to mind all the women who had chosen death rather than dishonour, and resolving to follow their example, she nevertheless goes out to face dishonour.

The characters in *The Franklin's Tale* are in fact ordinary human beings, neither very good nor very bad. They are not the conventional, idealised types the Franklin intended them to be. They break out of the mould in which he has set them. And the tale is much the better for this: the doings of conventional types are not really very interesting. We are offered instead the doings of realistic human beings, acting not from ideal principles but from the all-too-human motives of lust, shame, fear and greed.

Part 4

Hints for study

ONE OBVIOUS HINT is that the student MUST read *The Franklin's Tale* for himself. Reading these *Notes* is no substitute for reading the text! Furthermore, it is essential to read the text in Chaucer's own language, that is, in Middle English. There are various translations into modern English, and it is tempting to use one of them rather than the original text. This temptation should be resisted. It is impossible to translate poetry adequately into another language. This is particularly true when the poet relies as much as Chaucer does on ambiguities and subtle distinctions of meaning. These subtleties are lost in translation, but an examiner will be looking for a sensitivity to them in the student. Anyone attempting to write about *The Franklin's Tale* on the basis of study in translation is like someone attempting to write about a painting on the basis of examining a black-and-white photograph of it.

Chaucer's English is not as difficult as it may seem at first sight. It can be understood with a minimum of grammatical information. Rather than spending hours studying Middle English grammar, the student should begin immediately to read Chaucer. Where necessary, he may compare the text with the summary given in this book. He should not worry if at first, even with the aid of the summary, there are words and phrases which he cannot understand. As he reads, he will become more and more familiar with Chaucer's language, and many of his difficulties will vanish.

It may be useful to read the following notes on Chaucer's pronunciation and versification. With their aid it will be possible to read Chaucer with much greater facility.

Chaucer's pronunciation

Consonants

These were pronounced for the most part as in modern English. There were however no 'silent' letters in Chaucer's English. Thus the initial **k** was pronounced in words like *knit, knowe*; so was the **w** in *wrapped, wrecche, wreken, wreye* and so on. Sometimes **ssh** and **cch** are written where one would now write **sh** and **ch**: hence *wrecche, warisshed*. The pronunciation is as in modern English. **gh** was pronounced like **ch** in Scottish *loch* or German *nicht*.

Vowels

These were pronounced quite differently in Chaucer's time.

a could be either 'short' or 'long'.

Short **a**, as in *as, that, kan, Frankeleyn*, was pronounced as in modern English *hat*.

Long **a**, as in *tale, name, shame*, was pronounced as in modern English *father*, not as in modern *tale*. The length of this vowel is sometimes indicated (as in the examples given) by the presence of final –e; sometimes by writing **aa**, as in *baar, maad, taak*.

e could be 'short', 'long open', 'long close' or 'neutral'.

Short **e**, as in *beste, men, wel*, was pronounced as in modern English *bed*.

Long close **e** had a sound like that heard in modern *tale, paint*, or more exactly like the **é** in French *café*. It is found in *eek, seen*, and usually in words where the modern spelling is **ee**, like *fre*, 'free', *semed*, 'seemed', *seke*, 'seek'.

Long open **e** had a sound like that heard in modern *air, there*. Examples are *heep*, 'heap', *heed*, 'head' and most words where the modern spelling is **ea**.

Neutral **e** had a sound like **e** in modern *the* or **a** in modern *about*. Final **e**, that is, **e** on the ends of words, was usually not silent but was pronounced in this way; thus *wise, tale, name* all had two syllables in Chaucer's English.

i could be 'long' or 'short'.

Short **i**, as in *sit, in*, was pronounced just as in modern English *sit, in*.

Long **i** was pronounced as in modern English *machine*. Examples are *wise, emprise*.

Both the long and the short sound could also be spelt **y**: *lyk, stryf*, (long); *kyn, hym*, (short).

o could be 'short', 'long open' or 'long close'.

Short **o**, as in *hot, not*, was as in modern English *hot, not*.

Long open o was pronounced like **oa** in modern *broad*. Examples are *oon*, 'one', *hooly*, 'holy'. This is usually the pronunciation when the modern word is pronounced with the sound in *note, moat*.

Long close o was like the sound in modern *note*, but is found in words where the modern pronunciation is like **oo** in *doom*. Examples are *two, good*.

u could be 'short' or 'long'.

Short **u** was as in modern *full*. Examples are *burel, ful, humble*.

Long **u** was as in modern *rule*. It is usually spelt **ou**, as in *honour, resoun, labour*.

Diphthongs

ai—also written **ay, ei** or **ey**—was the sound of modern **i** in *die, sigh, I*. Examples are *Frankeleyn, Britayne, payne, maistrie, agayn, seyde*.

au—also written **aw**—was the sound of modern **ow** or **ou** in *how, ounce*. Examples: *obeysaunce, penaunce*.

oi—also written **oy**—was as in modern *join, boy*. Examples: *anoyeth, Troie, voyded*.

Versification

Chaucer uses the line most popular among later English poets, that is the *iambic pentameter* or ten-syllable line with alternating unstressed and stressed syllables (x = unstressed, ╱ = stressed):

> x ╱ x ╱ x ╱ x ╱ x ╱
> That pryvely she fil of his accord   (69)

It must be remembered that final –e was pronounced, and usually counted as an unstressed syllable:

> x ╱ x ╱ x ╱ x ╱ x ╱
> Men may so longe graven in a stoon   (158)

It does not *always* count as a syllable, however, and never does so when the next word begins with a vowel or an **h**:

> x ╱ x ╱ x ╱ x ╱ x ╱
> Sire, I wol be youre humble trewe wyf   (86)

It is permissible to have an extra, unstressed syllable at the end of a line, and this is very common:

x ╱ x ╱ x ╱ x ╱ x ╱ x

In Armorik, that called is Britayne   (57)

x ╱ x ╱ x ╱ x ╱ x ╱ x

She moorneth, waketh, wayleth, fasteth, pleyneth   (147)

We also find extra unstressed syllables within the line, the occasional omission of the first unstressed syllable, and frequently a less regular alternation of stressed and unstressed syllables than is indicated in the examples above. Very often the line begins with a stressed, rather than an unstressed syllable:

╱ x   x ╱ x ╱   x ╱ x ╱ x

He for his lady wroghte, er she were wonne   (61)

Chaucer is very free in his use of this line, and we should perhaps say no more than that he uses a line with five stressed syllables and a variable number of unstressed syllables.

Chaucer is, however, strict in his choice of rhymes. For Chaucer, words ending in –e do *not* rhyme with words without this ending. Thus *certeyn* rhymes with *seyn* but not with *atteyne* or *pleyne* (cf. lines 101–104). Most Middle English poets did not observe this distinction. Perhaps Chaucer's care in this respect reflects his reading of French poetry, where the same distinction was always maintained.

Preparing an examination answer

When you have read *The Franklin's Tale* through at least once and you are confident that you understand most of it, go through it carefully with the aid of the Summary and of the notes and glossary in your edition.

Have in your mind certain 'headings' which seem to be significant in the tale—for example, 'Characterisation', 'Convention', 'Love', 'Marriage', *'Trouthe'*, *'Gentillesse'*, *'Soveraynetee'*. Make a particular note of passages relevant to any of these headings.

Thus, the opening lines of the tale (lines 57–81) tell us about the Franklin's view of Love. Lines 72–80 are concerned with *maistrye* or *soveraynetee*. Lines 89–98 are again concerned with *maistrye*.

In the margin of your notebook, write a symbol against each note, using a different symbol for each heading. Suppose you use the letter **L** for Love, **S** for *Soveraynetee* (or *maistrye*, which is much the same thing), **Arv** for characterisation of Arveragus, **D** for characterisation of Dorigen, **Au** for characterisation of Aurelius, **F** for passages giving particular insight into the Franklin's own character, C for Convention, T for *Trouthe*, G for *Gentillesse*, and so forth.

The first page of your notebook might then look something like this:

Lines

F, G	1–36	The words of the Franklin to the Squire, etc. These reveal much about the Franklin himself, and particularly his interest in *gentillesse*
F	37–56	Again, these lines reveal much about the Franklin. Note his ostentatious use of RHETORIC—he strives to impress
L, C	57–81	Love, described in very conventional terms
S	72–80	*Soveraynetee*
G, T	81–88	*Gentillesse* and *Trouthe*

Copy out quotations from the text which you think may be useful to illustrate a point, but select ones which are short enough to commit to memory—more of this in a moment. Suppose you now wish to prepare an essay on a particular topic—say, 'Discuss the Franklin's views on the subject of *soveraynetee* in marriage'—you will find the relevant material easily by looking down your margin for all the S symbols. If you wish to answer the question, 'How much does *The Franklin's Tale* reveal about the Franklin's own character and opinions?' you will similarly find the relevant material by looking for the F symbols.

Selection and arrangement

Do not suppose, however, that you must use *all* the material relevant to a particular question. You will not be able to remember all the material in an examination. Even if you could remember it all, you will not have time to write it all down. And even if you could write it all down, your essay would be repetitive and disorderly. It is better to have in mind half-a-dozen of the major points, arranged not in the order they occur in the text, but in a logical order, so that your essay has a coherent structure, with a beginning, a middle and an end.

Quoting from the text

Do not attempt to memorise large passages of poetry in order to impress the examiner with your knowledge of the text. He will not be impressed:

he wishes to test your critical ability, not just your memory. Instead, quote short passages *relevant to the question you are answering*. The purpose of quoting is to justify your critical comments by reference to the text.

How not to quote

Suppose you were answering the question, 'Discuss the Franklin's views on *soveraynetee* in marriage.' Here is how *not* to proceed:

Early in his tale the Franklin says,

For o thyng, sires, saufly dar I seye,
That freendes everych oother moot obeye,
If they wol longe holden compaignye.
Love wol nat been constreyned by maistrye.
Whan maistrye comth, the God of Love anon
Beteth his wynges, and farewel, he is gon!
Love is a thyng as any spirit free.
Wommen, of kynde, desiren libertee,
And nat to been constreyned as a thral;
And so doon men, if I sooth seyen shal.

COMMENT: Here quotation has taken the place of discussion. The candidate has merely learned a passage by heart, and is displaying his knowledge without applying himself thoughtfully to the question. A very low mark!

The right way to quote

Here is the beginning of another answer to the same question, with a more intelligent use of quotation:

The Franklin is of the opinion that *soveraynetee* or *maistrye* has no place in marriage. He believes that 'Love wol nat been constreyned by maistrye.' When *maistrye* comes, he says, the God of Love beats his wings, 'and farewel, he is gon!' Accordingly the hero of his tale, Arveragus, agrees never to 'take no maistrye' over Dorigen against her will, 'But hire obeye, and folwe hir wyl in al.'

However it may be questioned whether Arveragus really does keep his promise in this respect. He orders Dorigen, much against her will, to keep her appointment with Aurelius: 'Ye shul your trouthe holden, by my fay!' And he forbids her, 'up peyne of deeth', ever to talk about the affair. This is hardly following her will in all things . . .

COMMENT: This candidate is selecting short, significant quotations to illustrate his points. In doing so he is showing just as much knowledge of the text as the other candidate, but is allowing himself more time for intelligent comment. High marks!

Answering the question

Obviously, the purpose of entering an examination is to try to answer the questions. Those who give a reasonable answer to the questions will pass, and those who do not, will fail. A surprising number of candidates, however, make no attempt at all to answer the questions. It may seem incredible that anyone should behave so foolishly, but they do. Many candidates in examinations write essays which are really 'non-answers'.

A non-answer

Here is a typical non-answer to the same question as before:

> The Franklin interrupts the Squire and tells him that he wishes his own son was like him and would mix with decent people and learn some *gentillesse* but the Host interrupts and asks the Franklin to tell a story and he says he will tell a Breton Lay apologises for his lack of skill in rhetoric and begins his story which is about a knight who loved a lady and served her and performed many labours in her honour until . . .

COMMENT: Believe it or not, this kind of non-answer is very common. The candidate is merely telling the story of *The Franklin's Tale*. He has not even read the question. He is very nervous and in his anxiety to write down all he knows about the tale is not stopping to think. This is why he uses no punctuation, but writes one long continuous sentence. Remember: there is no need to tell the story. The examiner will know it already.

Another non-answer

Here is another kind of non-answer, not as common as the previous one. The question again concerns the Franklin's views on *soveraynetee*:

> Chaucer's consummate artistry is manifested throughout the *Canterbury Tales* by his sophisticated technique of creating a microcosm of the macrocosm. The characters develop their own dimension of existence within a continuum of scintillating complexity. This exis-

tential tension is elaborated by all the technical resources at Chaucer's command, producing a radical dichotomy between subjective and objective reality. The German philosopher Heidegger has said . . .

COMMENT: This candidate has not read *The Franklin's Tale* at all, and has no idea how to go about answering the question. He knows that if he were to admit this honestly, he would fail the examination. So he tries to conceal his ignorance behind a veil of long, impressive words, and references to German philosophers. He hopes the examiner will be deceived, but this is most unlikely. This non-answer would gain even fewer marks than the previous one, which at least showed some knowledge of the story.

The technical term for this kind of writing is *waffle*. Do not waffle. Express your meaning plainly in simple words.

A hint on 'characterisation'

Examinations often contain a question on characterisation. If you answer one of these, it is not sufficient to write a character-sketch of the appropriate person. The character of, say, Dorigen, is not in itself of interest to the literary critic. What is of interest is Chaucer's technique in creating such a character. The question cannot be answered without consideration of the question of *irony*, for while the Franklin is saying one thing, Chaucer may intend us to see something different.

Suppose you were faced with the following question:

' . . . he was, if men sholde hym discryve,
Oon of the beste farynge man on lyve;
Yong, strong, right vertuous, and riche, and wys,
And wel biloved, and holden in greet prys.
Is there anything else to be said about Aurelius?

What is the examiner looking for here? First, he wants to see if you have observed that there is a difference between what the Franklin *says* and what we see happen in his tale. The Franklin says that Aurelius is *right vertuous*, but it does not necessarily follow that he is so.

Secondly, the examiner wants to see if you realise that these lines are of a very general and conventional nature. They could have been said about almost any squire in medieval literature. The Franklin is *trying* to create idealised, conventional figures. But he fails: Aurelius, like Arveragus and Dorigen, is not a conventional one-dimensional figure, but something more human: a mixture of good and evil, of base and noble, capable on the one hand of plotting to force his lady to love him, and on the other hand of a fine and selfless act of renunciation in the end.

A satisfactory answer to the question ought to contain these two points, clearly argued and supported by reference to the text.

Don't panic!

The above question could be phrased in a variety of ways. Here is the same question, or almost the same one, phrased differently:

> A scholar has recently written, 'Aurelius is little more than a rag-bag of courtly clichés . . . He loves, moans, suffers, pines, and wastes away in tactful silence, according to the rules . . .'
> Do you agree?

Alternatively, the question could be phrased in a quite straightforward manner:

> Discuss the characterisation of Aurelius.

So, if you find that the examiner has asked a question for which you feel unprepared, don't panic. Read the question carefully and think what it is that the examiner wants to know. It may be that he has asked a question for which you are very well prepared, but phrased it in a way you did not expect.

Some more characterisation questions

> 'The fresshe knyght, the worthy man of armes'—
> How much does this line tell us about Arveragus?

> ' . . . the treweste and the beste wyf
> That evere yet I knew in al my lyf.'
> Do you agree with this estimate of Dorigen?

Attempt answers to these questions, and then compare your efforts with the discussions of Arveragus and Dorigen in Part 3 of these *Notes*. Incidentally, when the question contains a quotation from the text, you would do well to show knowledge of where the quotation comes from, who says it and why. So if you were answering the question on Dorigen you might begin as follows:

> These lines are spoken by Aurelius when he sends Dorigen back to Arveragus after releasing her from her promise. They thus represent Aurelius's opinion of her. Since Aurelius is in love with Dorigen, and

since he is trying to comfort her after her grief, it is natural that he should say something favourable about her at this point. Nevertheless it is odd that he should praise her for being a 'true wife' when she has just met him for the very purpose of committing adultery . . .

Other examination questions

(a) 'Lordynges, this question, thanne, wol I aske now:
 Which was the mooste fre, as thynketh yow?'

 How would you answer this question?

(b) 'Who koude telle, but he hadde wedded be,
 The joye, the ese, and the prosperitee
 That is bitwixe an housbonde and his wyf?'

 Is the marriage between Arveragus and Dorigen a successful one? (HINT: *Distinguish here between whether the Franklin considers the marriage successful, whether Chaucer considers it successful, and whether you yourself consider it successful.*)

(c) 'Love wol nat been constreyned by maistrye'
 Discuss, with reference to *The Franklin's Tale*.

(d) Discuss the theme of *gentillesse* in *The Franklin's Tale*.

(e) 'Trouthe is the hyeste thyng that man may kepe.'
 Discuss the application of this view to *The Franklin's Tale*.

(f) Consider what light *The Franklin's Tale* throws on the Franklin's own character.

Some specimen answers

The following essays would be regarded as satisfactory answers to questions (a), (c) and (e) above. It is not intended that you should memorise them and serve them up in your own examination, but rather that you should use them as examples of what is acceptable and as a stimulus to your own thinking. They are not the only possible answers to the questions, and are perhaps not the best ones, but are all answers which could be produced within the limits imposed by an examination.

Question (a)
This question is asked by the Franklin at the end of his tale. He believes that his characters have acted in a *fre*, that is, a generous or noble,

fashion. The knight Arveragus has set aside his own feelings in order to send his wife Dorigen to keep her appointment with Aurelius. Aurelius in turn has sent her home untouched to Arveragus. He comments to the magician,

' . . . as frely as he sente hire me,
As frely sent I hire to hym ageyn.'

The magician in his turn has released Aurelius from his debt of a thousand pounds. So all three have, on the face of it, acted *frely*.

The Franklin is very concerned that his characters should act *frely*. He regards *fredom* or *franchise* (the two words mean much the same) as a great virtue, an important part of the *gentillesse* which he so much admires. He knows that *fredom* is a necessary part of a knight's character; his companion on the pilgrimage, the Knight, is renowned for 'Trouthe and honour, *fredom* and courteisie', and the Franklin is concerned to show that he himself is capable of understanding and displaying *fredom*. He does indeed display a kind of generosity: we discover in the General Prologue that there was always plenty to eat and drink in his house. But he overdoes it; he displays not true *fredom* but ostentatious gluttony. He displays in his own life a distorted kind of *fredom*, one might say a parody of *fredom*; and this is also the kind of *fredom* displayed in his tale.

Arveragus is not really *fre*. He is self-indulgent and irresponsible. Having taken on the responsibilities of marriage, he quickly grows bored with the life and leaves his wife for two years to indulge his hobby of jousting. He seeks only to 'lyve in ese' and for this reason promises never to exercise 'maistrye' over his wife against her will. He is quite unhelpful when Dorigen brings her problem to him, sending her off to keep her rash promise. This does not constitute generosity, but irresponsibility.

Chaucer draws our attention to the dubious quality of Arveragus' behaviour by his characteristic device (used to devastating effect in *Troilus and Criseyde*) of asking a question and failing to give a satisfactory answer. Perhaps many of us may consider Arveragus a 'lewed man' for putting his wife 'in juparite'. We must hear the tale before we condemn her. This avoids the question in two ways: first, the fact that the tale has a happy ending does not make Arveragus' action any less 'lewed' (stupid). And second, whether or not we condemn *her* is not at issue. The reader is left with an uneasy feeling that there is indeed something 'lewed' about Arveragus' behaviour.

Aurelius too is not really *fre*. Unlike Palamon in *The Knight's Tale* or the hero of Chrétien de Troyes' *Yvain*, who may be taken as classical examples of *franchise*, Aurelius is selfish, not caring what disgrace he brings on his lady, what mental anguish she suffers, so long as he can enjoy her body. It is true that in the end he prefers to forgo his 'rights'

Than doon so heigh a cherlyssh wrecchednesse
Agayns franchise and alle gentillesse;

and this is greatly to his credit. Nevertheless he is a very imperfect example of *fredom*.

Nor is the magician really *fre*. Again, he redeems himself at the end by generously releasing Aurelius from his debt; but up to this point he has been a shrewd enough bargainer:

He made it straunge, and swoor, so God hym save,
Lasse than a thousand pound he wolde nat have.

And he has been willing to take this money in return for bringing shame and distress to an innocent woman.

Dorigen also falls short of true *fredom*, when she is set against the heroic example of the noble ladies of olden times. She recalls all the *exempla* of noble women cited by Jerome in his *Adversus Jovinianum*, and concludes that the noble thing would be to kill herself. She fails however to do so.

Fre has another meaning, simply 'free'. Certainly the tale is much concerned with freedom, with binding and releasing. Dorigen apparently obtains a liberal régime, being proferred 'so large a reyne' by Arveragus. However, she soon has cause to complain of Fortune, 'That unwar wrapped hast me in thy cheyne'. Aurelius is confined to bed, caught in the snare of love; soon he too is ensnared in heavy debt. It is significant that both Aurelius and the magician talk of releasing their debtors from bonds:

I yow *relesse*, madame, into youre hond
Quyt every serement and every *bond* . . .

and

Sire, I *releesse* the thy thousand pound.

Chaucer was greatly interested in the theme of human freedom. In many of his works he explores the questions, How free are human beings? To what extent can they be said to possess free will, and to what extent are their destinies subject to external forces?

The external forces he saw as chiefly restricting human free will were social convention and planetary influence. Social convention assigned to each man—Knight, Squire or Scholar—his rôle in society, defined his character and limited his sphere of action. Planetary influences—that is, astrological forces—affected his character and the whole course of his life.

It is notable that the Franklin tries hard to create characters who are purely conventional types: Arveragus, the 'wise worthy knyght' who is 'of chivalrie the flour'; Aurelius the typical squire, 'Yong, strong, right vertuous, and riche, and wys'; Dorigen the perfect wife,

> ... the treweste and the beste wyf
> That evere yet I knew in al my lyf

as Aurelius calls her. The Franklin fails to give them any individualising characteristics, yet somehow they do manage to become credible human beings: they take on a life of their own, breaking out of the mould in which the Franklin has cast them. In this sense they become free, even of their creator the Franklin—though not of course of their ultimate cause, Chaucer himself.

It is notable too that astrology plays such a prominent part in the tale. It is by astrological forces that Dorigen is trapped in Fortune's chain. Perhaps in this sense the 'mooste fre' character is the magician, the astrologer who manipulates the forces which manipulate the other characters.

But the question is not intended to have a simple answer: it is intended rather to provoke reflection on the issues the Franklin has raised in the course of his tale, a tale which is full of unanswered questions, ambiguous motives and situations.

Question (c)

The Franklin is certainly of the opinion that 'Love wol nat been constreyned by maistrye', for having scarcely begun his story, he interrupts it with a lengthy digression maintaining that

> Whan maistrye comth, the God of Love anon
> Beteth his wynges, and farewel, he is gon!

Some scholars indeed have seen this as the theme of *The Franklin's Tale*. They maintain that *The Franklin's Tale* forms the conclusion of a 'marriage debate' begun by the Wife of Bath. She opens the debate by advocating the 'soveraynetee' (which means much the same as 'maistrye') of women in marriage. The Clerk counters by advocating the 'soveraynetee' of men, the Merchant describes a most disagreeable marriage in which neither partner trusts or respects the other, and the Franklin concludes with the description of an ideal marriage, based on mutual respect and forbearance.

Such at least is the theory. There is much that can, and has, been said both in support and in refutation of this theory. It suffices here to point out that the marriage of Arveragus and Dorigen is far from ideal, because the arrangement to which they come regarding the 'maistrye' will not bear the strain of a crisis. The arrangement is that Arveragus renounces his claim to 'maistrye':

Of his free wyl he swoor hire as a knyght
That nevere in al his lyf he, day ne nyght,
Ne sholde upon hym take no maistrye
Agayn hir wyl . . .

His renunciation of 'maistrye', however, is not absolute. He wishes to keep the outward appearance of 'maistrye':

> . . . the name of soveraynetee,
That wolde he have for shame of his degree.

Arveragus is trying to have it both ways. He wants to be both 'servant' and 'lord' to Dorigen—'Servant in love, and lord in mariage'. Chaucer draws attention to the paradox by describing it at some length; he is expert in the deliberate use of one or two lines more than a situation would seem to require. Here he uses the rhetorical device *expolitio* to state the same point six times in six consecutive lines:

Thus hath she take hir servant and hir lord,—
Servant in love, and lord in mariage.
Thanne was he bothe in lordshipe and servage.
Servage? nay, but in lordshipe above,
Sith he hath bothe his lady and his love;
His lady, certes, and his wyf also . . .

The suspicious reader may well feel that if a point needs to be hammered home six times, there must be something wrong with it. Chaucer plays on the reader's feeling of unease by describing this 'ideal' marriage in lines reminiscent of the highly ironic *Merchant's Tale*, and then adding a line which suggests that the 'ideal' situation was not destined to last:

Who koude telle, but he hadde wedded be,
The joye, the ese, and the prosperitee
That is bitwixe an housbonde and his wyf?
A yeer and more lasted this blisful lyf . . .

Arveragus's solution to the problem of resolving 'lordshipe' and 'servage' is to abdicate any responsibility in his marriage, indeed to absent himself from it. For most of the tale he is not physically present. His absence is the cause of Dorigen's problem in the first place. He has gone to

> . . . dwelle a year or tweyne
> In Engelond, that cleped was eek Briteyne.

Dorigen cannot at first discuss her situation with her husband, 'For out of town was goon Arveragus'. He is never around when he is needed. When he does return, he is of no use. His concern is not with Dorigen's feelings, but with his own reputation. Since, like the Franklin himself, he desires above all 'to lyve in ese', he acquiesces in Aurelius' dastardly scheme, taking care however to safeguard appearances and justifying his inaction with the fine principle, 'Trouthe is the hyeste thyng that man may kepe'. This only begs the question, 'What about the *trouthe* which Arveragus and Dorigen have sworn to each other?'

Aurelius, unlike Arveragus, sets out with some determination to 'constreyne' Dorigen to love him. He describes in great detail to Phebus a plan whereby he may enjoy Dorigen, and readily agrees to his brother's scheme whereby

> . . . moste she nedes holden hire biheste,
> Or elles he shal shame hire atte leeste.

This is blackmail. Aurelius does not concern himself with Dorigen's feelings. He is willing to humiliate her in order to gratify his passion. He attempts to trap her, to manipulate her, rather than allow her a free choice. It is significant that Aurelius turns to astrological forces to bring about his ends, for these forces were taken very seriously as determining, not only the outcome of events, but the characters of human beings. They were thus considered to be a major constraint on human freewill. Dorigen certainly feels that she has been trapped by forces greater than herself:

> 'Allas' quod she, 'on thee, Fortune, I pleyne,
> That unwar wrapped hast me in thy cheyne'.

Aurelius, then, lacks the submissiveness of the typical medieval lover. We might contrast him with Chrétien de Troyes's hero Yvain, who submits entirely to his lady's will. Aurelius feigns submission to Dorigen, using the conventional courtly language proper to lovers, but all the time insisting on his 'rights':

> Ye sle me giltelees for verray peyne.
> But of my deeth thogh that ye have no routhe,
> Avyseth yow er that ye breke youre trouthe.

The statement that 'Love wol nat been constreyned by maistrye' is self-evidently true. There is no way in which a man may force another person to love him. The obvious truth of the proposition is borne out by the fact that Aurelius's manoeuvres engender dismay and despair, not affection, in Dorigen. But to go to the other extreme and abdicate all responsibility is not the answer either. The Franklin does not succeed in his aim of portraying an ideal marriage, based on mutual forbearance.

Question (e)

This is the principle on which Arveragus acts when he sends Dorigen to keep her appointment with Aurelius. He places great value on *trouthe*, telling Dorigen 'Ye shul youre trouthe holden, by my fay!' He would rather 'ystiked for to be' than that Dorigen should fail to keep her *trouthe*.

By *trouthe* he means a solemn promise. He regards Dorigen's words, spoken 'in pley' to Aurelius, as constituting her 'trouthe'. Aurelius also takes her 'pley' in deadly earnest. In claiming his reward, he refers again and again to her jest as a solemn promise: 'Avyseth yow er that ye breke youre trouthe,' 'wel ye woot what ye han hight,' 'ye bihighten me,' 'youre trouthe plighten ye,' 'have your biheste in mynde.' When he releases Dorigen from her promise, Aurelius clearly uses the kind of language which would be appropriate to a solemn and binding contract:

I yow relesse, madame, into youre hond
Quyt every serement and every bond
That ye han maad to me as heerbiforn.

Two questions arise. First, are Aurelius and Arveragus being reasonable in taking Dorigen's careless banter so seriously? And second, even if a solemn promise was made, is Dorigen obliged to keep it?

To the first question it must be answered that Dorigen had, albeit in jest, used the word *trouthe*. If Aurelius can remove all the rocks, she says,

Thanne wol I love yow best of any man,
Have heer my *trouthe*, in al that evere I kan.

The 'rash promise' is a familiar motif in medieval literature. A character often makes a promise in jest, but is required to keep it in earnest. Thus, the hero of *Sir Gawain and the Green Knight* rashly promises to allow the Green Knight to strike him with an axe. So, within the conventions of medieval story-telling, it is natural that the promise should be taken seriously.

The second question is less easy to answer. It is of course important to keep a pledged word, but should one keep a promise to do something evil, such as committing adultery? Two wrongs do not make a right.

Furthermore, more than one solemn promise is made in *The Franklin's Tale*. Indeed, the tale is a network of promises. Arveragus, early in the tale, makes a promise to Dorigen:

Of his free wyl he swoor hire as a knyght
That nevere in al his lyf he, day ne nyght,
Ne sholde upon hym take no maistrie
Agayn hir wyl . . .

Likewise, Dorigen promises Arveragus

Sire, I wol be youre humble trewe wyf;
Have heer my *trouthe,* till that myn herte breste.

Likewise Aurelius also gives a solemn promise to the magician: 'Ye shal be payed trewely, by my *trouthe*.' And the magician in turn gives his word to Aurelius: 'have heer my feith to borwe.' Aurelius takes his promise seriously: 'My *trouthe* wol I kepe, I wol nat lye.' And he tells the magician, 'I failled nevere of my trouthe as yit.' The magician asks, 'Have I nat holden covenant unto thee?' and he releases Aurelius from his promise in the same exaggerated terms as Aurelius had used in releasing Dorigen:

Sire, I releesse thee thy thousand pound,
As thou right now were cropen out of the ground,
Ne nevere er now ne haddest knowen me.

There is thus a series of solemn promises binding the various characters together: Aurelius and Dorigen; Dorigen and Arveragus; Aurelius and the magician. The problem arises when one promise conflicts with another. Dorigen has given her *trouthe* to Arveragus to be his 'humble trewe wyf.' This oath implies that she will be faithful to him, not taking any other man as a lover. In keeping her *trouthe* to Aurelius, she is thus breaking her previous, and far more solemn, *trouthe* to Arveragus. Similarly Arveragus has sworn to Dorigen never to exercise dominion over her against her will. Yet this is exactly what he does, in making Dorigen, against her will, keep her *trouthe* to Aurelius.

Arveragus and Dorigen can keep one promise only by breaking others. 'Trouthe is the hyeste thyng that man may kepe' is a fine principle, but very difficult to put into practice.

Part 5

Suggestions for further reading

Editions of *The Franklin's Tale*

SPEARING, A.C. (ED.): *The Franklin's Prologue and Tale*, Cambridge University Press, Cambridge 1966. This is the best and most recent edition available and is strongly recommended.

HODGSON, PHYLLIS (ED.): *Chaucer: The Franklin's Tale*, The Athlone Press, London, 1960. Older than Spearing's edition but useful for its discussion of Chaucer's use of Boccaccio and of the Astronomy, Astrology and Magic of the tale.

Chaucer's other works

The best way to gain a deeper understanding of *The Franklin's Tale* is to read more widely among Chaucer's other works, especially the rest of *The Canterbury Tales*. The best edition is

ROBINSON, F.N. (ED.): *The Works of Geoffrey Chaucer*, second edition, Oxford University Press, London, 1957.

Less expensive, and very useful for the beginner, is

CAWLEY, A.C. (ED.): *Chaucer: The Canterbury Tales*, Everyman's Library, Dent, London, 1958. This reprints the text from Robinson's edition, without the learned notes but with translations of difficult words and phrases on the same page as the original. This makes it a very easy text for rapid reading, though the book does not provide the information necessary for detailed study.

Scholarship and criticism

CURRY, W.C.: *Chaucer and the Mediaeval Sciences*, second edition, Allen and Unwin, London, 1960. Standard treatment of astrology.

DONALDSON, E.T.: *Speaking of Chaucer*, The Athlone Press, London 1970. A very good book on Chaucer, though it does not discuss *The Franklin's Tale* itself.

HUSSEY, M., SPEARING, A.C. and WINNY, J.: *An Introduction to Chaucer*, Cambridge University Press, Cambridge, 1965. A useful basic introduction.

MATHEW, G.: *The Court of Richard II*, John Murray, London 1968. Survey of literature, art, politics of Chaucer's time. Good background reading.

MILLER, ROBERT P.: *Chaucer: Sources and Backgrounds*, Oxford University Press, New York, 1977. The source of *The Franklin's Tale* is given on pages 121–35.

The author of these notes

W.G. EAST was educated at Reading School, Keble College, Oxford, and Yale University. His doctoral research was on the famous twelfth-century historical novelist Geoffrey of Monmouth. He has taught Middle English in the National University of Ireland and at the Centre for Medieval and Renaissance Studies at Oxford.

He is now in Holy Orders, but continues to publish in various areas of medieval literature, including Chaucer and Geoffrey of Monmouth.

York Notes: list of titles

CHINUA ACHEBE
Things Fall Apart

EDWARD ALBEE
Who's Afraid of Virginia Woolf?

ANONYMOUS
Beowulf
Everyman

W. H. AUDEN
Selected Poems

JANE AUSTEN
Emma
Mansfield Park
Northanger Abbey
Persuasion
Pride and Prejudice
Sense and Sensibility

SAMUEL BECKETT
Waiting for Godot

ARNOLD BENNETT
The Card

JOHN BETJEMAN
Selected Poems

WILLIAM BLAKE
Songs of Innocence, Songs of Experience

ROBERT BOLT
A Man For All Seasons

HAROLD BRIGHOUSE
Hobson's Choice

ANNE BRONTË
The Tenant of Wildfell Hall

CHARLOTTE BRONTË
Jane Eyre

EMILY BRONTË
Wuthering Heights

ROBERT BROWNING
Men and Women

JOHN BUCHAN
The Thirty-Nine Steps

JOHN BUNYAN
The Pilgrim's Progress

BYRON
Selected Poems

GEOFFREY CHAUCER
Prologue to the Canterbury Tales
The Clerk's Tale
The Franklin's Tale
The Knight's Tale
The Merchant's Tale
The Miller's Tale
The Nun's Priest's Tale
The Pardoner's Tale
The Wife of Bath's Tale
Troilus and Criseyde

SAMUEL TAYLOR COLERIDGE
Selected Poems

SIR ARTHUR CONAN DOYLE
The Hound of the Baskervilles

WILLIAM CONGREVE
The Way of the World

JOSEPH CONRAD
Heart of Darkness

STEPHEN CRANE
The Red Badge of Courage

BRUCE DAWE
Selected Poems

DANIEL DEFOE
Moll Flanders
Robinson Crusoe

WALTER DE LA MARE
Selected Poems

SHELAGH DELANEY
A Taste of Honey

CHARLES DICKENS
A Tale of Two Cities
Bleak House
David Copperfield
Great Expectations
Hard Times
Oliver Twist
The Pickwick Papers

EMILY DICKINSON
Selected Poems

JOHN DONNE
Selected Poems

GERALD DURRELL
My Family and Other Animals

GEORGE ELIOT
Middlemarch
Silas Marner
The Mill on the Floss

T. S. ELIOT
Four Quartets
Murder in the Cathedral
Selected Poems
The Cocktail Party
The Waste Land

J. G. FARRELL
The Siege of Krishnapur

WILLIAM FAULKNER
The Sound and the Fury

HENRY FIELDING
Joseph Andrews
Tom Jones

F. SCOTT FITZGERALD
Tender is the Night
The Great Gatsby

GUSTAVE FLAUBERT
Madame Bovary

E. M. FORSTER
A Passage to India
Howards End

JOHN FOWLES
The French Lieutenant's Woman

JOHN GALSWORTHY
Strife

MRS GASKELL
North and South

WILLIAM GOLDING
Lord of the Flies
The Spire

OLIVER GOLDSMITH
She Stoops to Conquer
The Vicar of Wakefield

ROBERT GRAVES
Goodbye to All That

GRAHAM GREENE
Brighton Rock
The Heart of the Matter
The Power and the Glory

WILLIS HALL
The Long and the Short and the Tall

THOMAS HARDY
Far from the Madding Crowd
Jude the Obscure
Selected Poems
Tess of the D'Urbervilles
The Mayor of Casterbridge
The Return of the Native
The Woodlanders

L. P. HARTLEY
The Go-Between

NATHANIEL HAWTHORNE
The Scarlet Letter

SEAMUS HEANEY
Selected Poems

ERNEST HEMINGWAY
A Farewell to Arms
The Old Man and the Sea

SUSAN HILL
I'm the King of the Castle

BARRY HINES
Kes

HOMER
The Iliad
The Odyssey

GERARD MANLEY HOPKINS
Selected Poems

TED HUGHES
Selected Poems

ALDOUS HUXLEY
Brave New World

HENRIK IBSEN
A Doll's House

HENRY JAMES
The Portrait of a Lady
Washington Square

BEN JONSON
The Alchemist
Volpone

JAMES JOYCE
A Portrait of the Artist as a Young Man
Dubliners

JOHN KEATS
Selected Poems

PHILIP LARKIN
Selected Poems

D. H. LAWRENCE
Selected Short Stories
Sons and Lovers
The Rainbow
Women in Love

HARPER LEE
To Kill a Mocking-Bird

LAURIE LEE
Cider with Rosie

CHRISTOPHER MARLOWE
Doctor Faustus

HERMAN MELVILLE
Moby Dick

THOMAS MIDDLETON *and*
    WILLIAM ROWLEY
The Changeling

ARTHUR MILLER
A View from the Bridge
Death of a Salesman
The Crucible

JOHN MILTON
Paradise Lost I & II
Paradise Lost IV & IX
Selected Poems

V. S. NAIPAUL
A House for Mr Biswas

ROBERT O'BRIEN
Z for Zachariah

SEAN O'CASEY
Juno and the Paycock

GEORGE ORWELL
Animal Farm
Nineteen Eighty-four

JOHN OSBORNE
Look Back in Anger
WILFRED OWEN
Selected Poems
ALAN PATON
Cry, The Beloved Country
THOMAS LOVE PEACOCK
Nightmare Abbey and *Crotchet Castle*
HAROLD PINTER
The Caretaker
SYLVIA PLATH
Selected Works
PLATO
The Republic
ALEXANDER POPE
Selected Poems
J. B. PRIESTLEY
An Inspector Calls
WILLIAM SHAKESPEARE
A Midsummer Night's Dream
Antony and Cleopatra
As You Like It
Coriolanus
Hamlet
Henry IV Part I
Henry IV Part II
Henry V
Julius Caesar
King Lear
Macbeth
Measure for Measure
Much Ado About Nothing
Othello
Richard II
Richard III
Romeo and Juliet
Sonnets
The Merchant of Venice
The Taming of the Shrew
The Tempest
The Winter's Tale
Troilus and Cressida
Twelfth Night
GEORGE BERNARD SHAW
Arms and the Man
Candida
Pygmalion
Saint Joan
The Devil's Disciple
MARY SHELLEY
Frankenstein
PERCY BYSSHE SHELLEY
Selected Poems
RICHARD BRINSLEY SHERIDAN
The Rivals

R. C. SHERRIFF
Journey's End
JOHN STEINBECK
Of Mice and Men
The Grapes of Wrath
The Pearl
LAURENCE STERNE
A Sentimental Journey
Tristram Shandy
TOM STOPPARD
Professional Foul
Rosencrantz and Guildenstern are Dead
JONATHAN SWIFT
Gulliver's Travels
JOHN MILLINGTON SYNGE
The Playboy of the Western World
TENNYSON
Selected Poems
W. M. THACKERAY
Vanity Fair
J. R. R. TOLKIEN
The Hobbit
MARK TWAIN
Huckleberry Finn
Tom Sawyer
VIRGIL
The Aeneid
ALICE WALKER
The Color Purple
KEITH WATERHOUSE
Billy Liar
EVELYN WAUGH
Decline and Fall
JOHN WEBSTER
The Duchess of Malfi
OSCAR WILDE
The Importance of Being Earnest
THORNTON WILDER
Our Town
TENNESSEE WILLIAMS
The Glass Menagerie
VIRGINIA WOOLF
Mrs Dalloway
To the Lighthouse
WILLIAM WORDSWORTH
Selected Poems
WILLIAM WYCHERLEY
The Country Wife
W. B. YEATS
Selected Poems